64 9
ATC

MW01166878

Shaping the Next Generation

David & Elaine Atchison

FIRST BAPTIST CHURCH LIBRARY
TUCKER, GEORGIA

LifeWay Press
Nashville, Tennessee

✠

© Copyright 1998 • LifeWay Press

All rights reserved

ISBN 0-7673-3476-0

Dewey Decimal Classification: 649
Subject Heading: PARENTING

This book is the text for course CG-0430 in the subject area
Home/Family in the Christian Growth Study Plan.

Unless otherwise indicated, Scripture quotations are from the NEW AMERICAN
STANDARD BIBLE, © Copyright the Lockman Foundation, 1960, 1962, 1963,
1968, 1971, 1972, 1973, 1975, 1977, 1995
Used by permission.

Scripture quotations marked (NIV) and in "31 Daily Petitions" are from
the Holy Bible, *New International Version*, copyright © 1973, 1978, 1984
by International Bible Society.

Printed in the United States of America

LifeWay Press
127 Ninth Avenue, North
Nashville, Tennessee 37234

FIRST BAPTIST CHURCH LIBRARY
TUCKER, GEORGIA

Contents

Meet the Atchisons

David and Elaine founded and lead Disciple's Call, a teaching and writing ministry that focuses on making disciples. David and Elaine want couples and families to develop the oneness only possible by centering every relationship on Jesus Christ. Their style of teaching is creative, informal, and transparent. Everything they share is from truths in God's Word that have impacted their own lives.

David draws from his background as a businessman who has experienced both the successes and failures of competing in the marketplace. He has been a leader in many areas of ministry, including speaking and teaching; designing and leading worship; and writing, directing, and performing drama.

Elaine works part-time as a pediatric speech-language pathologist in a local hospital in Nashville. She also writes for Disciple's Call and other Christian publications. David and Elaine co-wrote the devotional guide *Divine Appointments*. They live in Franklin, Tennessee, where their ultimate ministry is parenting twin boys, Blake and Joel, and their daughter, Amanda.

Introduction

Is it really possible to shape a generation? To significantly influence its values and direction? Some might speculate that our culture and its societal trends are the primary influences on a generation. The breakdown of the family and a mobile generation have caused many young parents to seek resources outside their families for help in child rearing. In fact, the trend is to allow day care, school, even church programs to assume the primary role in shaping the child. God intends for parents to fulfill this role. Jonathan Edwards was one man who believed he could make a difference.

Jonathan Edwards was a pastor, writer, and later, president of Princeton University. Born in 1703, he and his wife had 11 children. Of his known descendants, there were:

- 14 presidents of colleges
- more than 100 college professors
- more than 100 lawyers
- 30 judges
- 60 physicians
- more than 300 clergymen, missionaries, and theology professors
- 60 prominent authors

There is scarcely any great American industry that has not had one of his family among its chief promoters. Such is the product of one American Christian family who built a heritage that has lasted for generations.

Exodus 20:5 speaks of the punishment for sin being passed on to the "third and fourth generation," but in Exodus 20:6 we learn that God's grace extends much further than His wrath! The reward for righteousness is passed on to "a thousand generations." Even though Jonathan Edwards was known for his rigorous and demanding schedule of studying, teaching, writing, and pastoring, he placed a high priority on his family. He came home and spent an hour each day with his children. In leaving his legacy and heritage, he proved that godly traits have a greater impact than our human weaknesses and inadequacies.[1] Whether we realize it or not, we are shaping the next generation. It will be our children and their children who will reflect the extent of our personal investment in future generations.

Being the parents of twin sons and a daughter can be an exciting, exasperating, and ecstatic experience—all in one day. We knew God gave us children to shape their character, but we missed one of the most important principles of parenting: God wants to mold our character as well! Over the years, we have discovered over 230 verses of Scripture providing a treasure chest of wisdom from which to draw. Parents need a "big picture" for biblical parenting that will inspire them to explore independently. Your role—and ours—is not to portray perfect parents, but fellow guides who are traveling the same road on the awesome journey called *parenting*. As you prepare for this study, will you commit to take practical steps to strengthen your family? We pray that God will bless you and expand your vision for what He wants to accomplish through you while *Shaping the Next Generation*.

—David and Elaine

---

[1]Adapted from Dr. Winship as quoted by J. Oswald Sanders, *A Spiritual Clinic* (Chicago: Moody, 1958), 90.

How to Use This Book

Welcome to *Shaping the Next Generation*! By choosing to participate in this study, you are demonstrating your commitment to apply biblical principles and instill godly character in your children.

The heart of *Shaping the Next Generation* is contained in the video segments. This book supports that material. As you work through this book, there are several terms you will encounter. Your study will make more sense if you become familiar with those terms ahead of time.

Parent View—A viewer's guide to be used while watching the video segments.

Parent Talk—Discussion questions based on the material in each video segment. These questions can be used in a small-group meeting at your church, in a home, or in another setting in your community. They can also be used one-on-one with your spouse or another parent.

Parent Shaper—A personal study section expanding the content of each video segment. This material is to be used after Parent View and Parent Talk. You will benefit more by working through this section over several days.

Parent Project—Practical activities to use with your children.

As you begin your study of *Shaping the Next Generation*, consider the following suggestions. Each one will make your study time more meaningful for you and your family. Check the box by those you will commit to follow.

- ❑ Ask the Holy Spirit for guidance; commit to be obedient to what He teaches you.
- ❑ Spend time in earnest prayer both alone and with others.
- ❑ Spend time meditating on and discussing with others what God is revealing to you.
- ❑ Keep a journal of what the Lord is teaching you. In years to come, the journal will remind you of things your memory won't.
- ❑ Expect God to honor your faithful obedience to Him.

To gain the most from *Shaping the Next Generation*, it is important that you participate in all parts of the study. View each video segment, participate in the discussion with a small group or another individual, spend time in personal study, and carry out the projects outlined at the end of each chapter. These parts are designed to challenge you and to help you draw application from what God has to say.

May God bless you in your study as you seek to join Him in *Shaping the Next Generation*.

Chapter 1
Precious in His Sight

PARENT VIEW 1

We are not experts in parenting but we can learn from God—the ultimate expert, the model parent—through His Word.

⌂ Key Principle 1

SCRIPTURE USED DURING THE VIDEO SESSION ...
Hebrews 11:23
1 Samuel 16:7
Psalm 127:3-5

We have a brief _____ of _____ to

shape the next generation.

The Families of Moses and Samuel

1. God's _____ was on their children before they had

any idea how they would _____ their generation.

2. Both families _____ God and their

_____ was solidly grounded in Him.

3. They took advantage of those _____ and most

_____ years.

⌂ Key Principle 2

If we focus on the _____ _____ for our

children we lose sight of _____ _____

for the next generation.

7

The Bank of Human Worth[1]

1. Gold Coin of _____

2. Silver Coin of _____

3. Bronze Coin of _____

⚠ Key Principle 3

When we focus on _____ _____ for our

children, He will use us to shape generations to come.

• Behold, children are a _____ of the Lord.

• The fruit of the womb is the _____.

• Like _____ in the hand of a warrior, so are the

children of one's youth.

An arrow must be:

_____

_____

_____

CONTRASTING …

CULTURAL LENS	AND	BIBLICAL LENS
Limited: our vision		Infinite: God's vision
Focus: outer person		Focus: inner person
Leads to performance building		Leads to character building
Liabilities, risks, "feathers"		Gifts, rewards, arrows
Goal: survival		Goal: victory

Parent Talk 1

Use the following as a guide to talk with your spouse, another parent, or group of parents. Pray together as you begin your discussion.

1. As children many of us dreamed of what our own kids would be like, but never as much as during pregnancy or when anticipating adoption. No wonder people say, "We're expecting!" Recall some of your dreams or fantasies about parenthood from anytime B.C. (before children).

2. I wonder if any of us fully realized the "more and less" that children bring when they burst into our world! Brainstorm as many answers as possible for these statements (write them below and then share them):

Children mean more ...

- _____
- _____
- _____
- _____
- _____

Children mean less ...

- _____
- _____
- _____
- _____
- _____

3. Which of your childhood experiences do you hope to duplicate with your children? Which experiences do you hope to avoid?

4. Some common dreams parents have for their children include exceptional beauty, great importance, unusual intelligence, athletic or material success, popularity, high achievement, and good health. Unmistakably, our dreams are not always God's plans. How have your dreams differed from reality?

5. Review the chart at the end of Parent View 1. Would you describe the family in which you grew up as primarily "cultural" (world's lens) or "biblical" (God's lens)? Explain your response. How do you view your family today?

Parent Shaper 1

Every Christian parent wants the best for his or her children. The difficulty lies in knowing what is best for them! We can be sincere in our intentions and still miss our opportunity to raise our children according to God's vision. The Bible tells about three sets of parents who took advantage of the limited time they had to influence their children.

MOSES

Lovely in the Sight of God

Read Exodus 1:22 and Hebrews 11:23.

Amram and Jochebed were pointed out as faithful parents in Hebrews' "Hall of Faith" (see Hebrews 11:23). From the moment of his birth, there appeared in Moses something extraordinary (see Acts 7:20-22). It seemed by his countenance that the beauty of the Lord rested upon him. Just at the time when Pharaoh's cruelty reached its height, God sent His deliverer into that generation. Today, many couples hesitate to bring children into such a troubled world. Who knows which children God has chosen to bring needed hope and change to this generation. By faith, like Moses' parents, we can raise our children in any cultural or political climate. The calling belongs to us. The plan belongs to God. Faith in Him will overrule any fear we have.

☼ **What do you consider to be the greatest threat to your child's welfare?**

_____

_____

_____

Then Pharaoh gave this order to all his people: "Every boy that is born you must throw into the Nile, but let every girl live" (Exodus 1:22).

By faith Moses, when he was born, was hidden for three months by his parents, because they saw he was a beautiful child; and they were not afraid of the king's edict (Hebrews 11:23).

Released to God

Read Exodus 2:1-10 in your Bible.

Sooner than most, Amram and Jochebed had to release their
son. However, they provided him with a water-resistant basket
which served as an "ark of salvation" in the Nile River. Once
Moses was beyond their protection, the Lord kept Moses from
danger, and His plan was grander than any parent could devise!
Besides preserving Moses' life, God provided a way for Moses'
parents to continue influencing him during his early childhood.
Though he was adopted by Pharaoh's daughter and raised in
luxury by learned teachers, his earliest influences held strong.

☼ **What kind of "ark" are you building to prepare your
child for his release into the world?**

_____

A Transfer of Vision: The Deliverer

Read Hebrews 11:24-27.

Whenever I hear "nightmare" statistics, I think, *Those aren't our
kids.* Josh McDowell and Bob Hostetler, in *Right from Wrong,*
woke me up. Their study of the beliefs and lifestyle choices of
3,795 active church youth from 13 denominations revealed
major confusion about what the "right thing" is. For example:
- 1 in 6 measured right vs. wrong by whether it works.
- 1 in 8 accepted breaking the law if it doesn't harm others.
- Almost 1 in 5 (19 percent) of 11 to 12 year olds believed it is
  always or sometimes OK to have sex.[2]

Purposeful attempts to influence our children's values must not
be put off until they enter the high school youth group! When
Moses weighed the worst of following God against the best of
the world, he chose God. Who introduced Moses to the Living
God? Where did he gain such vision? When was he instructed in
the faith if he was raised in the Egyptian palace?

☼**If you knew your window of influence was small, what
would you do differently to influence your children?**

_____

_____

By faith Moses, when he had grown up, refused to be called the son of Pharaoh's daughter; choosing rather to endure ill-treatment with the people of God, than to enjoy the passing pleasures of sin; considering the reproach of Christ greater riches than the treasures of Egypt; for he was looking to the reward. By faith he left Egypt, not fearing the wrath of the king; for he endured, as seeing Him who is unseen (Hebrews 11:24-27).

❦Inside Look

Children say the funniest things that open a window to their hearts. In third grade Blake told his teacher he couldn't wait until sixth grade, when he could "digest" a frog. Amanda picked up a withered flower and said, "Poor little flower is scared to death." At four, Joel asked one of those questions that leaves parents speechless: "How old was Jesus when he knew he was God?" How does the saying go? Out of the mouths of babes!—*Elaine*

♥**Inside Look**

I will never forget how sick I felt when Elaine called me long distance to tell me our eight-year-old boys had been exposed to illegal, hard-core pornography. They had been playing with a group of boys in a drainpipe in our neighborhood and found magazines with pictures of perversions our eyes could not even interpret. We had worked so hard to guard their eyes and maintain their innocence! I drove all night to get home and address the confusion and nausea they felt every time they remembered what they saw. As it turned out, that horrible experience opened the door for our ongoing conversations about God's plan for sexuality and man's capability to pervert it. That was six years ago, and one boy recently commented that for the first time, he cannot consciously bring those images to mind. I shudder to think of all the children who are exposed to such things on a regular basis.—*David*

SAMUEL

"Asked of the Lord"
Read 1 Samuel 1:19-23 in your Bible.
Elkanah and Hannah grasped God's vision for their child but had a limited time of influence. If you are not familiar with the heart-wrenching story of Hannah's infertility, go back and read the first part of 1 Samuel 1. How they dealt with those years was a testimony of their marriage and faith in God. When their prayer for a child was finally answered, Hannah did not forget that she had dedicated her only son for a lifetime in the Lord's service. She knew her time with him was short; historians give a range of three to eight years. The family continued in their strong faith, and Hannah took her time with Samuel seriously. She went annually to the temple, even though she was not under obligation; however, now she chose to stay with the little boy. She knew the time would come all too quickly when she would not have him so near.

⚙**How do you protect time with your child given personal demands, media, school, friends, etc?**

_____

_____

Released to God
Read 1 Samuel 2:12-21 in your Bible.
Suddenly Samuel was thrust into an atmosphere where God's holiness was being mocked in the temple. His character is contrasted with Eli's older sons who were judged by God as "worthless men who did not know the Lord." (Later we will explore Eli's parenting and Samuel's calling.) Although Samuel performed behind-the-scenes tasks, the word *ministered* speaks of his devotion to God in the way he performed those tasks. What set him apart from the compromising family that adopted him? How did he remain strong during such impressionable years? The answer can be found in 1 Samuel 2:21.

☼Compare 1 Samuel 2:21 with Luke 2:52. What will set your child apart when he faces compromising situations?

_____

_____

God's Spokesman in His Generation
Read 1 Samuel 3:19-21 in your Bible.

God honored Samuel by revealing Himself and speaking to others through him. Samuel became both famous and useful to God as a prophet, a circuit judge, even a city manager. He anointed Saul and David as kings, and was set apart from others because of his industrious service, intense devotion, and power in prayer. Samuel was also listed among the greatest heroes of the faith (see Hebrews 11:32-34). God loved Moses and Samuel. In another generation, Jeremiah was pleading for sinful Judah for the third time when God said: " 'Even though Moses and Samuel were to stand before Me, My heart would not be with this people' " (Jeremiah 15:1). We can only imagine His affection for parents who play such a role in preparing their children for the next generation!

☼What can we learn from Moses' and Samuel's parents to prepare our children to confront negative influences they will face?

_____

JESUS

Hope of Every Generation
Read Luke 1 and 2 in your Bible.

Moses foreshadowed the Messiah. Samuel foretold the Messiah. Jesus fulfilled the hope of every generation since creation. No parents were ever given a clearer picture of God's vision for their child than Joseph and Mary. Even before Jesus' birth, they were told His true origin and identity. Still, they didn't know God's timing or manner of revealing His Son. Jesus grew up as other children, in body and mind, but with extraordinary spirit

The boy Samuel grew before the Lord (1 Samuel 2:21).

Jesus kept increasing in wisdom and stature, and in favor with God and men (Luke 2:52).

FIRST BAPTIST CHURCH LIBRARY
TUCKER, GEORGIA

And it came about that after three days they found Him in the temple, sitting in the midst of the teachers, both listening to them, and asking them questions. And all who heard Him were amazed at His understanding and His answers (Luke 2:46-47).

Have this attitude in yourselves which was also in Christ Jesus, who, although He existed in the form of God, did not regard equality with God a thing to be grasped, but emptied Himself [laid aside His privileges], taking the form of a bond-servant (Philippians 2:5-7).

and wisdom beyond His years. Whether or not Jesus knew He was God as a youth, He subjected Himself to His parents' care and influence. We know that the image of God that shone from within was apparent by age 12 (read Luke 2:46-47)! This is why parents must focus their expectations on the "inner person" rather than appearance and achievement alone.

⚙️**Is it reasonable to expect that your child could be wise beyond his or her years by the end of childhood? What would it take? Pray about this now.**

Jesus, the Selfless Servant
Read Philippians 2:5-7.
Jesus laid aside the privileges of being God for our sakes. He should have been treated like a prince, but His life was one of humility and humiliation. Jesus chose to be obedient to God's calling for Him; and knowing that the essence of God is good, He poured out His very life for us. Paul's dramatic encounter with Jesus changed the rest of his life. Regardless of the demands, Paul remained content in every condition of life, from prosperity to affliction. But, Paul didn't do it alone; it is beyond our human strength to remain content in every condition.

⚙️**You may struggle with the desire to be in control when it comes to selfLESS parenting demands. If you are not content today, what can you do to overcome your greatest discouragement?**

_____

_____

Two Choices
Read Philippians 4:11 and 2 Corinthians 4:8-9,16 in your Bible.
No one has to remind a parent that child rearing requires daily attitude adjustments! According to Philippians 4:11, even in circumstances we can't control, there are always choices within our control. Someone once said, "Pain is inevitable. Misery is optional." As we meet the challenges of parenting, we can choose to adjust to our circumstances in two ways: willingly or

FIRST BAPTIST CHURCH LIBRARY
TUCKER, GEORGIA

unwillingly. One way or the other, we will adjust! In 2 Corinthians 4:16, *renewed* means "refreshed, feeling young again"! Our great God can accomplish that miracle even when our exhausted bodies cannot!

When life's a zoo, remember the woman who telephoned a friend to ask how she was feeling:

"Terrible!" came the reply. "My head's splitting, the house is a mess, and the kids are simply driving me crazy!" Sympathetically the caller said, "Listen, go and lie down. I'll come over right away and clean up the house, and take care of the children while you get some rest. By the way, how is Sam?" "Sam?" the complaining housewife gasped. "Who is Sam?"

"My heavens," exclaimed the first woman, "I must have dialed the wrong number!" There was a long pause. "Are you still coming over?" the harried mother asked hopefully.[3]

Have you ever felt like parenthood is harder than you thought it would be?

☼**In the margin we have contrasted the phrases in 2 Corinthians 4:8-9. First, read the negative portion of each phrase—"afflicted, perplexed, etc." Next, read the positive portions—"not crushed, not despairing, etc." Circle the set that best describes your attitude.**

A New Outlook
Read Psalm 139:1-24 and Psalm 56:8 in your Bible.
Are you focusing so closely on being a parent that you've forgotten you are God's child? Psalm 139 reminds us that God's vision of His children is perfectly clear. Because God is present everywhere, He knows all. Because God made us, He knows us. Our children are the work of His hands—the birth parents are the instruments. Parents were His work as well. We have never been alone from the moment of our conception, however isolated we may feel. What vision God has for you! "Five year-old Matthew saw that there was only a little chocolate milk left in the carton, so he announced: 'Mom, I'm going to have to drink this all myself because there's not enough for Christine, too.' Dad overheard this and said sternly, 'Matthew, if Jesus were

🖤Inside Look
Before Amanda was born, we were given a blurry little black and white ultrasound photo that was barely recognizable as a baby, yet God had written all the days that were ordained for her in His book before one of them came to be (see Psalm 139:16). He already knew about the day she would have kidney surgery, and when she hemorrhaged after her tonsillectomy. Recalling such sovereignty was all that comforted me on many occasions when I couldn't recognize how the circumstances could be part of His good plan for our lives.—*Elaine*

We are afflicted in every way ... perplexed ... persecuted ... struck down OR
"We are ... not crushed ... not despairing ... not forsaken ... not destroyed (2 Corinthians 4:8-9).

*Though hast taken account
of my wanderings;
Put my tears in Thy bottle;
Are they not in Thy book?
(Psalm 56:8).*

🦁Inside Look

Elaine and I have always
been very involved in the
churches where we have
been, and we were
determined that children
would not change that.
When our children were still
preschoolers, we wrote and
directed the drama for a
Christmas program (or was
it Easter? They all run
together!). What I do
remember is that we were
constantly farming the kids
out so we could work on the
play, the scenery, etc. We
were pleased that the kids
never complained about all
the different places we left
them, until one of our five
year olds came running to
Elaine with the news of the
century: "Mom! Mrs. Smiley
made us cookies today—in a
pan!" We both realized that
we needed to spend a little
more time with our
children!—*David*

here, what would He do?' Without hesitating, little Christine
answered for him: 'If Jesus were here, He'd make more chocolate milk!' "⁴

⚙️**Recall your most difficult parenting days. When did
you feel most empty or inadequate to be a parent?
What does Psalm 56:8 tell you about the God you
serve?**

_____

_____

Allow God to "Refill" You
Read Isaiah 35:3 and 2 Corinthians 12:14-15 in your Bible.
There will be days you will feel there isn't enough of you to go
around and you have nothing more to give. Jesus modeled the
principle of "emptying" ourselves and "taking the form of a
servant." If we will look to Him, He will "refill" us so we can
invest our lives in our children. Our children's attitudes will be
influenced by the attitudes we adopt, the expectations we have,
and the choices we make. Even Christian parents can choose to
believe that parenting is merely a lesson in survival, but God has
far greater confidence in us. May we all have the vision to raise
young champions as we seek to shape the next generation for
Christ. To some of you, it may seem the next generation is a long
way off, but it's not! Every day we make generation-changing
differences. A wise man once said, "Children are the living
messages we send to a time we will not see." What a tremendous
blessing to know our children have the potential to achieve
things we will never be able to accomplish. Our only chance to
be a true mom or dad is right now—not when we are asking
ourselves the age-old question: "Where did the years go?"

⚙️**As you end this session, take a few minutes to sit
quietly before the Lord. Reread your responses
throughout this section. Tell God your cares. Ask Him
to renew you—refresh you—and refill you with His
vision and the strength to meet your holy calling as a
parent. Then look forward to this new day—a fresh
start knowing that God has already seen it all!**

Parent Project 1

1. Even though we have witnessed an effort to reclaim strong family values, there is still a large gap between cultural and biblical views of the family. How have you "bought into" the cultural view of children? (e.g. unnecessary liabilities, risks, performance building). Pay attention to the messages you see and hear this week. Keep a notepad handy to record your observations. At the end of the week, determine ways you can uplift biblical values and confront cultural values your family faces.

2. It is natural for parents to have high hopes and expectations for their children, but dreams can become demands when motives are wrong. As you interact with your children this week, evaluate your expectations:
   • How do I emphasize performance building more than character building?
   • Why do I want my child to reach the goals I have set for him/her?
   • Are my expectations and goals fitting for my child?
   • Am I encouraging—or forcing—my child to "reach for the stars"?
   • How age-appropriate are my expectations?

3. Pick out three different days this week to share object lessons you create to illustrate Psalm 127. Find creative ways to let your children know they are gifts, rewards, and arrows.

4. Only God knows what will happen every day of our lives. Nothing that has happened or will happen to us or to our children takes Him by surprise. Spend a few minutes in prayer each morning and evening this week releasing your child to God.

---

[1] Adapted from James Dobson, *Hide or Seek* (Old Tappan, NJ: Fleming H. Revell Company, 1974).

[2] Josh McDowell and Bob Hostetler, *Right from Wrong* (Dallas: Word, 1994), 254-63.

[3] Bobby Moore, "Any Old Port in a Storm," *First Baptist Informer* (Mineral Wells, TX: First Baptist Church, May 13, 1981).

[4] *Focus on the Family* (October 1986).

Chapter 2
Repairing and Building a Family Heritage

PARENT VIEW 2

Our "baggage" not only affects us, it affects our children as well. Our family backgrounds affect our parenting.

⛪ Key Principle 1

The God-given needs for _____ and

_____ influence both _____ and

_____.

The Model of Jesus

Open heart = _____

Open ears = _____

Open arms = _____

SCRIPTURE USED DURING THE VIDEO SESSION ...
Philippians 3:13-14
Mark 10:13-16
Exodus 20:6
John 8:32
Colossians 3:13
1 John 3:1
Joel 2:25

🏠 Key Principle 2

The secret to breaking down _____ barriers is

applying _____ and _____ to past

experiences.

🏠 Key Principle 3

God is the _____ _____ and will build

a new _____ for future _____ of your

family.

ARE YOU ...

SHAPING A HERITAGE? OR	HINDERING A HERITAGE?
Open heart: time	Closed heart: neglect
Open ears: attention	Closed ears: preoccupation
Open arms: affection	Closed arms: lack of affection
Result: security, intimacy	Result: insecurity, isolation
Impact: Generational freedom	Impact: Generational chains
Rx: Truth and blessing	Rx: Truth and forgiveness

Parent Talk 2

Use the following as a guide to talk with your spouse, another parent, or group of parents. Pray together as you begin your discussion.

1. What baggage have you carried into your parenting? What is your most positive childhood memory? Most negative? Most embarrassing? Think about it for a few minutes and then share each memory.

2. Of all the millions of "tapes" in your brain, why do you think you still remember the ones you do? Memories before age eight can be very enlightening, because later we begin to apply reason and logic to our experiences. What is your earliest memory? Begin when you were in elementary school and work backward. Share one or two that stand out in your mind.

3. Read through the list below. What was the general atmosphere in your home during childhood? Circle those that apply. What factors do you think contributed to that atmosphere?

Authoritarian	Materialistic	Critical
Permissive	Loving	Stressful
Perfectionistic	Warm	Giving
Competitive	Secure	Happy
Hurried	Open	Strong
Overprotective	Insensitive	Optimistic

4. How did your parents give you the blessings of time, attention, and affection?

5. Which blessing—time, attention, affection—does your child need most from you today? (If you have more than one child, answer the question for each one.)

6. Complete these statements:
   I know my parents love(d) me when they …
   Sometimes I question(ed) my parents' love when they …

Parent Shaper 2

G od desires that all His children receive "the blessing." As parents, we are called to pass that blessing on to our children. This week we will look at the origin of the blessing and learn how we can pass that blessing on to our children.

First Modeled by God

Read Genesis 12:2-3 and Galatians 3:6-14 in your Bible.
The first reference to *blessing* was God's charge to His new creation: "And God blessed them; and God said to them, 'Be fruitful and multiply' " (Genesis 1:28). After the flood, God blessed Noah and his sons in the same way (Genesis 9:1). Abram received a more extensive blessing that included all of us. This promise was a crown over all the others because it pointed to Jesus, the greatest blessing the world ever received. Galatians goes on to say that all believers are "sons of Abraham," and recipients of the blessing God spoke thousands of years ago.

Parents Pass on the Blessing

Read Genesis 27 and Hebrews 11:20-21 in your Bible.
In the Old Testament, blessing children took faith, because parents were verbalizing the future of their children and grand-children, knowing they would not live to see it. Both Jacob and Esau received a blessing from Isaac, and Jacob later blessed grandsons Ephraim and Manasseh as if they were his own. Generation by generation, this special charge was passed from parent to child. In *The Blessing*, Gary Smalley and John Trent outline the five elements of the blessing found in Scripture: 1) meaningful touch, 2) the spoken word, 3) the expression of high value, 4) the description of a special future, and 5) an active, genuine commitment to the person.[1]

And I will make you a great nation,
And I will bless you,
And make your name great,
And so you shall be a blessing;
And I will bless those who bless you,
And the one who curses you I will curse.
And in you all the families of the earth shall be blessed (Genesis 12:2-3).

♥Inside Look
My mom had a special way of verbalizing her faith in God's great plans for her kids. Many times she would pray with me about what God might call me to be or about the girl I would someday marry. Even now, she seems to know just when I need a card or phone call that reconfirms her love and commitment to me.—*David*

☼Which elements of the blessing did you receive as a child? Circle the number by each one (p. 21). Were they given by ❑ your parents or ❑ another important adult? Check one. Which elements were not received during your childhood? Underline that one (or those).

God Blesses His Children
Read Isaiah 44:1-5 and Proverbs 10:22 in your Bible.
Billy Graham, the world-renowned evangelist, recalled his earliest childhood memory of his father: "It was in the afternoon. I remember him clapping his hands, opening his arms, calling 'Billy Frank, come to Daddy! C'mon to Daddy, Billy Frank!' "[2] We can appreciate how this exceptional man of God discovered a loving and caring Father whose arms are opened wide! But, not everyone receives approval from their earthly parents. Many spend a lifetime seeking it. Only God's blessing can fill the void even loving parents cannot fill. Generations before Jesus was born, God spoke of His great love which draws us to become his sons and daughters. Though our earthly parents may have fallen short, we can be assured that our heavenly parentage is secure.

☼How does God's blessing reach beyond the blessing of earthly parents?

_____

_____

God Knows Your Past
Read Matthew 18:5-6,10 and Psalm 34:15-19 in your Bible.
Sadly, there are parents whose pride, ambition, and selfishness lead them to neglect, even abuse the ones who long for their blessing. Many of them never received a blessing from their parents, either. Jesus warned about respecting the personhood of others and clearly stated the extreme penalty for those who hinder or harm "little ones." It is comforting to know that God's angels are individually assigned to protect our children. Throughout Scripture, God acknowledges those who have been troubled, crushed, or brokenhearted by others. God affirms that in His timing, even the memory of them will be "cut off."

It is the blessing of the Lord that makes rich,
And He adds no sorrow to it (Proverbs 10:22).

See that you do not despise one of these little ones, for I say to you, that their angels in heaven continually behold the face of My Father who is in heaven (Matthew 18:10).

✷**Looking back on your childhood, what persons or negative experiences cannot seem to be "cut off" from your memory? List two or three of them.**

_____

_____

Take the Past to God

Read Lamentations 3:40 and John 8:32,36 in your Bible.
God says we need to stop. Quit all that running, slow down, and come to Him so He can talk to us and reason with us. Ample time must be devoted—using our minds and spirits over our emotions—to analyze the past from God's viewpoint. Jesus provided a balanced path to both insight and healing. True disciples know and continue in His Word, and the key to freedom is to apply truth to our lives. Many are caught right here, because they have never learned what God's Word really says. Hebrews 4:12 describes its power as living, active, sharp, piercing, able to judge everything—even memories we have carefully buried or hidden for many years.

✷**How have you applied God's Word to the persons or past experiences you listed above?**

_____

_____

Stuck Between Past and Future

Read Matthew 5:9,44; 6:12-15; and 2 Corinthians 5:18-20 in your Bible.
After appropriate intervention, an abused youngster is left to make sense of the past, grieve the loss, and get on with life. After tears and counseling, everyone reaches the same crisis point. The most difficult step for every victim or survivor is crossing the giant chasm called *forgiveness*. Some spend hours imagining how God will annihilate the offender, then when nothing happens, all hope is lost. Some decide God doesn't care or even exist. Our judicial hearts tend to rate insults by how unforgivable they are, but a search of Scripture will not turn up

For the word of God is living and active. Sharper than any double-edged sword, it penetrates even to dividing soul and spirit, joints and marrow; it judges the thoughts and attitudes of the heart (Hebrews 4:12, NIV).

♥Inside Look

When my grandfather died, my parents gave me his Bible. It was a treasure to find a note I had written him 10 years earlier, nestled near the Scripture verses I had shared in my letter. Without a word, I received a precious blessing that spoke volumes about my significance to him.—*Elaine*

Now all these things are from God, who reconciled us to Himself through Christ, and gave us the ministry of reconciliation (2 Corinthians 5:18).

any transgression beyond God's forgiveness. We are charged to demonstrate a higher standard than showing kindness only to those who treat us well (even unbelievers do that). God commands us (the offended) to ask Him to forgive the offender and cause them to be at peace with us. The task continues. We must bless, or speak well of them, and actively do good to them. God calls reconciliation a ministry, knowing only He can mature and equip us for such a supernatural response.

☼**Which of the commands in these verses have you followed toward your offenders? Which is the most difficult to obey?**

_____

_____

How blessed is he whose transgression is forgiven, Whose sin is covered! How blessed is the man to whom the Lord does not impute iniquity, And in whose spirit there is no deceit! (Psalm 32:1-2).

How Can I Forgive?
Read Psalm 32:1-2; Psalm 103:10-12; and Romans 2:4 in your Bible.
How happy and humbled we are to realize that our debts to God have been paid in full by the extravagant sacrifice of Jesus Christ! He didn't wait until we felt bad enough, or tried to pay Him back, or deserved it. He didn't drive us to repentance, but drew us by persistently loving us. We tend to excuse and downplay our sins against God as "mistakes" or "slip-ups." We too easily forget the extreme measures God took to release us and wipe away our offenses toward Him. We also exaggerate the smallest insults from others, elevating them as equal with sinning against God Himself. And how do we respond to them? *How can I forgive?* The answer is tough, but clear. We have no choice in the matter. God commands us to release our enemies to His justice if we ever hope to be released from our own pain. That seems so backwards in a dog-eat-dog, eye-for-an-eye world, but God's ways are often opposite of human reasoning.

"Blessed are you who weep now, for you shall laugh" (Luke 6:21).

How Can I Forget?
Read Isaiah 61:1-10 and Luke 4:18; 6:21 in your Bible.
Jesus was the fulfillment of Isaiah's prophesy about healing. A friend shared with me one way she has dealt with recurring memories already released to God. As a little girl, she witnessed

her mother being severely beaten by her father. Years later, while praying with a group of women, she pictured Jesus sitting with her on the stairs. She imagined Him holding her hand and comforting her mother, whom He had clothed with clean robes. Now when the memory replays, she views it differently. A severely wounded person has a terrible time imagining the possibility of freedom from the unpredictable ambush of painful memories. Look how close the two words are. To *forgive* is a gift only God can enable us to give. To *forget* is a gift only God can enable us to receive. When we release our past offenders, God will begin the process of restoring our future.

☼Who will you release to God today? What memory do you most desire to forget? Pour out your heart to God.

Remembering to Forget
Read Isaiah 49:14-16 in your Bible.
Sometimes it is a slow process to break the chains that hold us to the past. In *Kids Who Carry Our Pain*, Robert Hemfelt and Paul Warren wrote, "A behavior problem displayed by a child is at least three generations in the making. … Everything occurring in a family, regardless of how carefully it may be hidden, impacts the children. Everything."[3] That sounds a lot like what God said in Exodus 20:5-6! One way to take major steps forward is to replace old messages and memories with God's truths from Scripture.

☼Match one of the following verses to counter one of the negative messages on the right.

Galatians 4:7	You'll never change.
Colossians 7:12	You're worthless.
Philippians 1:6	No one will love you.

Applying the medicine of truth to our past experiences gives us a whole new outlook on the wonderful heritage God has planned for us, because "we are inscribed on His hands!"

What About the Present?
Read Mark 10:13-16; Matthew 19:13-15; and Luke 18:15-17 in your Bible.
Centuries before Jesus was born, the prophet Isaiah described

♥An Inside Look
Every time I see Necco Wafers, I remember visiting my grandparents in Marlin, Texas, and how my bare feet felt on the cool, hardwood floors of Pinno's store. My other grandmother lived nearby and often baby-sat my sisters and me. One evening, when I was especially talkative, she said she wished I was a television so she could turn me off. Today I completely understand how she felt, but for some reason that memory still plays back when I am feeling inadequate or insecure about others' acceptance.—*Elaine*

"The power of Satan is in the lie. The power of the believer is in knowing the truth." —Neil Anderson, *The Bondage Breaker*[4]

❤️**An Inside Look**

Three recollections from my younger years:

- When I was four, I clearly remember everyone's panic when my mother was bitten by a snake at the lake. I can still see myself standing beside her bed during the year it took her to recover.
- My dad was a pastor and was often called away in the evenings. I remember trying to stay awake until he got home so I could tell him good night.
- In our little house, my bedroom opened directly into the kitchen. I can recall the feeling of waking up early on Sunday mornings and lying in my bed watching Dad study his Bible before leaving to preach.—*David*

the gentleness of the Messiah. "In His arm He will gather the lambs, and carry them in His bosom" (Isaiah 40:11). Jesus modeled God's intention of blessing children. The children who were brought to Jesus did not need healing and were not old enough to be taught; yet, their parents valued them enough to believe that Christ's blessing was important. Jesus was displeased that the disciples discouraged the children from approaching Him. Jesus not only encouraged, but ordered that time be set aside for them. No adult agenda—even "ministry"— was too important to neglect the little ones. Picture Jesus stopping everything to gather the littlest ones onto His lap, to listen to their giggles and questions, and to bless them with His tender words and gentle touch. God calls us to model that same pattern for our children.

☀️**How approachable are you? Describe how you can improve your approach to children with an open heart, open ears, and open arms.**

_____

_____

Beware of Returning to the Past

Read James 3:8-10 and 1 Peter 3:8-9 in your Bible.

In *Putting Away Childish Things*, David Seamonds said, "A lot of folks like to dig around in their past and find excuses for their present behavior."[5] Have you become a perfectionist? A controller? A workaholic? A rageaholic? It shows great inconsistency to praise God for His deliverance, then turn upon others. Like flukes of nature, sarcasm, criticism, harshness, or put-downs are not consistent with God's grace. Why do we seem to find the restraint to speak respectfully to strangers, but can't control lashing out at those we love the most? It may take some time and input from others to consistently demonstrate how much you truly care for your family. Don't give up! Mark Twain once said, "I can live two months on a good compliment." The growing seeds of your time, attention, and affection will blossom and change your child's family tree.

Make the Most of Today

Read Psalm 128 and Psalm 90:12 in your Bible.

We never know what small thing in our eyes will be remembered or how it will impact our children. A successful attorney said, "The greatest gift I ever received was a gift I got for Christmas when my dad gave me a small box. Inside was a note saying, 'Son, this year I will give you 365 hours—an hour every day after dinner. It's yours. We'll talk about what you want to talk about. We'll go where you want to go, play what you want to play. It will be your hour!' My dad not only kept his promise, but every year he renewed it—and it's the greatest gift I ever had in my life. I am the result of his time."[6] Taking time daily to affirm each family member yields benefits that cannot be measured.

God Will Take Care of the Future

Read Ephesians 1:3-14; Romans 8:15; and Jeremiah 29:11 in your Bible.

It is time for the years of destruction and brokenness to be restored. We are no longer slaves to the past, so there is nothing in the future to fear. God says we were chosen to be His children. We have been permanently adopted as sons and daughters, making intimacy with our Heavenly "Abba" (Daddy) a reality. He has reserved the best blessings for His children, and has great plans for us today. What God is doing now is nothing in comparison to all He desires for our futures. In Christ, we are royal heirs—princes and princesses of the King of Kings. As Oswald Chambers often remarked, "We're spoilt bairns of the Almighty!"[7] Paul gave our marching orders: "One thing I do: forgetting what lies behind and reaching forward to what lies ahead, I press on" (Philippians 3:13-14).

☼**Close this chapter by thanking God for the blessings He has lavished on you and asking God for a vision of the future He has planned for you and your descendants.**

A righteous man who walks in his integrity—How blessed are his sons after him (Proverbs 20:7).

♥Inside Look
I still cry when I watch *Father of the Bride*, because I desired that kind of relationship during childhood. When our daughter first watched the film, she began to sob uncontrollably. When she finally composed herself, she vowed, "Dad, I will never get married and leave you!" and burst into tears again. What a great picture of breaking the chains of the past. My tears were for what can never be relived. Hers were for what God has already restored!—*Elaine*

"Then I will make up to you for the years That the swarming locust has eaten" (Joel 2:25).

Parent Project 2

1. Couples may want to reflect on the following questions individually, then discuss them with their spouses. Single parents will want to find a trusted friend or family member to share with. Problems that were years in the making may require a period of counseling with a fellow Christian.
   - What is the heaviest bag you carry today or have "unpacked" recently?

neglect	what ifs	guilt	fear of failure
criticism	abuse	rejection	disappointment

   other(s): _____
   - What needs to be done with it now?

2. Steve Farrar debates the supposition of quality versus quantity time in *Point Man*: "Quality time comes at the most unusual moments. You never know when it will happen. It usually makes an appearance some place in the realm of quantity time."[8] Chart how much "quantity time" you average with your child each day then rate the quality of it. You may need to divide up the day into a.m., p.m., and evening. Ask your child to help you set up a point system for rating quality.

	Quantity Time Spent	Which Parent?	Quality Rating
Monday	_____	_____	_____
Tuesday	_____	_____	_____
Wednesday	_____	_____	_____
Thursday	_____	_____	_____
Friday	_____	_____	_____
Saturday	_____	_____	_____
Sunday	_____	_____	_____

3. Write a blessing for your child (include an apology, if needed). Then share it with them. Try to include each of elements of the blessing.

[1]Gary Smalley and John Trent, *The Blessing* (Nashville: Thomas Nelson, 1986), 35-97.
[2]Kevin Leman and Randy Carlson, *Unlocking the Secrets of Your Childhood Memories* (Nashville: Thomas Nelson, 1989), 188.
[3]Robert Hemfelt and Paul Warren, *Kids Who Carry Our Pain* (Nashville: Thomas Nelson, 1990), 68-70.
[4]Neil T. Anderson, *The Bondage Breaker* (Eugene: Harvest House, 1990), 23.
[5]Kevin Leman and Randy Carlson, *Unlocking the Secrets of Your Childhood Memories* (Nashville: Thomas Nelson, 1989), 20.
[6]*Sermons Illustrated* (Holland, OH: Jeff and Pam Carroll, May 1989).
[7]David McCasland, *Oswald Chambers: Abandoned to God* (Grand Rapids: Discovery House, 1993), 183.
[8]Steve Farrar, *Point Man* (Portland: Multnomah, 1990), 26.

Chapter 3
Shaping Character by Design

PARENT VIEW 3

⌂ Key Principle 1

God has chosen _____ to be _____

_____ along with Him.

The only _____ that will stand is a _____

in Jesus Christ.

⌂ Key Principle 2

God's _____ are the _____

for character building.

Some Attributes of God

- _____ (Luke 1:37)

- _____ (Matthew 11:29)

- _____ (John 16:33)

- _____ (Ephesians 2:10)

SCRIPTURE USED DURING THE VIDEO SESSION ...
1 Corinthians 3:9-13
Deuteronomy 6:5-7
Hebrews 5:14
Philippians 4:8

Courage
The ability and tenacity to take risks.

Integrity
Honesty in every reguard. Doing what is right whatever the cost.

Wisdom
Seeing life from God's perspective and applying God's truth to each decision in life.

Unselfishness
Consider others more important than yourselves.

Discernment
The ability to distinguish between right and wrong, truth and error.

Love
A deep love for God reflected on to others should be the trademark of every Christian home.

Moral Purity
Uncompromising in living according to God's standards.

Perseverance
Never quit what you begin until the purpose has been fulfilled.

Teachable
A strong appetite for learning new truth and a willingness to receive constructive criticism.

⌂ Key Principle 3

We must capture _____ _____ to build character.

Teachable moments are those _____ times when our kids are _____ and _____ and _____ to receive and hear _____ _____ taught to them.

Philippians 4:8 Test
• Is it true?
• Is it honorable?
• Is it just?
• Is it pure?
• Is it lovely?
• Is it gracious?
• Is it excellent?
• Is it worthy of praise?

ARE YOU BUILDING A ...

GODLY PERSON	OR A	GOOD CITIZEN
Goal: Character		Goal: Performance
Roots: Parent's convictions		Roots: Parent's preferences
Source: God's power		Source: Human effort
God's attributes		Worldly attributes
Love of Christ		Love of man
Filled: fullness of God		Empty: futility of man

Parent Talk 3

Use the following as a guide to talk with your spouse, another parent, or group of parents. Pray together as you begin your discussion.

1. Imagine the days when your children will be old enough to leave home. What character qualities will they need most? Brainstorm qualities by listing them below and then discuss why each one is important.

   _____   _____

   _____   _____

   _____   _____

   _____   _____

2. What character qualities seem to be in short supply among young people today? Why do you think these qualities are missing? What negative impact is the absence of these qualities having on our culture?

3. Who (or what) was the greatest character shaper in your life? How intentional was that training?

4. Which character traits will be easiest for you to pass on to your children? Why?

5. Which character traits will be most difficult for you to pass on to your children? Why?

6. How balanced are you in your emphasis on physical, intellectual, social/emotional, and spiritual development? Which area do you tend to overemphasize? Underemphasize? What steps can you take to bring more balance?

*Unless the Lord builds
the house,
They labor in vain who
build it;
Unless the Lord guards
the city,
The watchman keeps awake
in vain (Psalm 127:1).*

❦Inside Look

My sister lived in a neighborhood where a man in a golf cart gave citations if the grass was too long or the flower beds needed weeding. Most of the families were totally wrapped up in this whirlwind of possessions and activities. A house down the street was being remodeled, and I stopped to admire the work that had come to a standstill. I didn't know that a few weeks earlier, one of their children had been killed in a car accident. The change in the neighborhood was dramatic. Suddenly, what was happening inside houses mattered more than the way the outside looked.—*Elaine*

Parent Shaper 3

Can you imagine being Jesus' parents? Luke 2:39 says they did "everything according to the Law of the Lord." The result was a balanced, complete child by early adolescence. It is important to neither overemphasize nor neglect any area of character building. We must pray, asking the Lord to make us aware of every character-building opportunity and to guide us in equipping our children to become wise adults.

A High Calling—Wise Master Builders
Read 1 Corinthians 3:7-13 in your Bible.
Christian parents are engaged in God's business. It is an honorable calling to work under His watchful eye. Only God can cause the growth. We cannot afford to be indifferent about how we build. The only solid foundation for character building is a relationship with Jesus Christ. Without that, it will be extremely difficult to accomplish other character goals. Consider the building materials listed. Gold, silver, and precious stones are not easy to acquire because they must be mined from deep within the earth. Because of their lasting value, some will give up everything to find them. On the other hand, wood, hay, and straw are abundant and right on the earth's surface. They are gathered quickly but also wither, burn up, or blow away easily. God says each builder's work will ultimately be displayed and tested for its true value.

⚙**List the character building materials you have been using in your parenting. Circle those you consider wood, hay, and straw. Underline those you consider gold, silver, or precious stones.**

_____

_____

A Wise Person or a Good Citizen?

Read Jeremiah 9:23-24 in your Bible.

There has been a lot of press both locally and nationally about teaching values to children. Everyone wants respectful, responsible, law-abiding children. What never seems to be resolved is, "Whose values will we teach?" Whether you are a wise person or just a good citizen has its roots in your convictions and preferences. Convictions are values that withstand time, persecution, even death. Preferences are values we prefer until someone changes our mind, or disagrees, or threatens our next promotion. A good citizen boasts in his wisdom, strength, and achievements, while a wise person boasts in what God has done. A good citizen measures herself by others, while a wise person measures herself by God. *Truth* is defined as "fidelity to an original or standard." In *Right from Wrong*, Josh McDowell asserts that God's nature and character define truth—He is the original. It doesn't matter what we think, but who God is.[1]

Write a sentence summarizing your standard for settling claims about right and wrong.

_____

_____

How Can I Build Another's Character?

Read Ephesians 3:14-21 in your Bible.

We can work on building the physical and intellectual strength of our children, while leaving them spiritual weaklings. Their love for God will take root and become established as they see their parents rooted and established in Christ. Helping them explore the exceeding greatness of His love is best supported by a community of devoted Christians. God uses grandparents, teachers, even coaches as character builders. How high should our expectations be? We should expect that they "may be filled up to all the fulness of God" (Ephesians 3:19). Parents also need God's filling to pass on godly qualities to their children. In John 14:26, Jesus promised that "the Helper, the Holy Spirit, whom the Father will send in My name, He will teach you all things, and bring to your remembrance all that I said to you." Don't you feel better knowing He is there to empower you for the task?

Inside Look

"Jimmy Stories" were born out of constant turmoil over caring for toys. One night I created a simple tale about a boy with a treasured toy that was ruined after he left it outside. The children not only connected with the parable, they began reminding each other about Jimmy! These stories became a ritual and provided an easy vehicle for many other character lessons. Elaine achieved a similar result with dolls and puppets. Characters like Waldo the Whiner or Casey the Crab could portray negative qualities in a non-threatening way that penetrated their minds and hearts more effectively than lecture number 458 ever could!
—*David*

Now to Him who is able to do exceeding abundantly beyond all that we ask or think, according to the power that works within us, to Him be the glory (Ephesians 3:20-21).

Capturing Teachable Moments

Read Deuteronomy 6:6-9 in your Bible.

Teachable moments are the framework for character training in everyday situations. Teachable moments are defined as neutral times when observations, stories, character studies, word pictures, or object lessons naturally occur. The best teachable moments often occur in the middle of a game, at breakfast, in the car, on walks, or during bedtime rituals. Not every character lesson has to be a scheduled, structured time of instruction. In fact, most aren't! Whether "in your house" or "by the way," in the morning or at bedtime, God expects us to have His words etched on our hearts so we won't miss the multitude of character building experiences around us! Integrity can be taught during a tennis game. Discernment can be taught choosing television programs. Diligence can be taught weeding the garden. Courage and perseverance can be taught on a hike. Self-discipline can be taught making beds or buying clothes. Consideration can be taught in the restaurant. The possibilities are endless when we are paying attention! Centuries ago, God revealed the secret to writing His commandments on the heart—it's not a list, or a lesson, but a lifestyle.

⚙**Identify two teachable moments that came your way this past week.**

_____

_____

A Character Manual for All Generations

Read Proverbs 1:8-9 and 1 Thessalonians 2:11-12.

Until his later years, Solomon was world-renowned for wisdom. He had prayed for it as a young man. Kings and seekers traveled long distances to consult with him. Solomon spoke over 3,000 proverbs in his lifetime. About 800 are found in the book of Proverbs. Their purpose was to give young people the skills and discipline to act with wisdom, discernment, and discretion. These sayings were taught in riddles, figures, and practical illustrations from daily life, and were passed along from adult to child each generation. Through the centuries, parents have used stories, poems, and fables that teach character qualities.

*Hear, my son, your father's instruction,
And do not forsake your mother's teaching;
Indeed, they are a graceful wreath to your head,
And ornaments about your neck (Proverbs 1:8-9).*

*You know how we were exhorting and encouraging and imploring each one of you as a father would his own children, so that you may walk in a manner worthy of the God who calls you into His own kingdom and glory
(1 Thessalonians 2:11-12).*

Bill Bennett compiled hundreds in his anthology titled *The Book of Virtues.* The key is to teach character qualities in vivid ways that children can relate to.

A Developmental Growth Chart for Character
Read 2 Peter 1:3-9 and Romans 8:29 in your Bible.
How do toddlers learn character qualities? The same way they learn to run—first they take baby steps. Peter reminds us that when we became Christians, God gave us "everything pertaining to life and godliness" (2 Peter 1:3), but it takes a lifetime for our character to fully unfold. This passage cites an eight-part developmental progression. Faith in Christ is number one. When His Spirit controls our lives, we begin to grow in moral excellence, knowledge, self-control, perseverance, godliness, brotherly kindness, and love. These character qualities are not the exception, but are to be possessed by all Christians "and are increasing." Our inspiration to pursue these qualities and model them for our children is because they will render us both useful and fruitful in every area of our lives!

☼**List in the margin the character qualities found in 2 Peter 1:5-7. Place a check by the qualities you possess. Circle the ones that are increasing. Pray that God will increase each of them in your life, so you can build them into your children's lives.**

Preparing to Build
Read 2 Timothy 2:15.
A young lumberjack asked a logging crew foreman for a job. The foreman replied, "Well, let's see if you're good enough to work for me." The young man stepped forward and skillfully cut down a large tree. The foreman was impressed and said, "You can start on Monday!" Monday, Tuesday, Wednesday, then Thursday rolled by. On Thursday afternoon the foreman approached the young man. "You can pick up your paycheck on your way out today. We're letting you go because you've fallen behind. You were in first place on Monday but dropped to last by Wednesday." The young man objected, "But I'm a hard worker! I arrive first, leave last, and even work through my break times!" The foreman considered the situation for a moment. "Have you been sharpening your axe?" he asked. The

If these qualities are yours and are increasing, they render you neither useless nor unfruitful (2 Peter 1:8).

F _____

P _____

M _____ E _____

G _____

K _____

B _____ K _____

S _____ -C _____

L _____

Be diligent to present yourself approved to God as a workman who does not need to be ashamed, handling accurately the word of truth (2 Timothy 2:15).

🌼**Inside Look**
Before kids, I spent as much time as I wanted journaling prayers and studying Scripture. When we had three in diapers, they would cry about the time I got settled. It took persistence to grab time alone, much less time alone with the Lord! I learned God is available at any moment. Rocking a baby at 4:00 a.m. became an opportunity to pray for each child. Oswald Chambers' devotional book was by the bathtub, a prayer journal waited on the nightstand, and Bible verses were by the sink when abbreviated visits with God presented themselves.—*Elaine*

Activity is often the anesthetic to deaden the pain of an empty life.
—Howard Hendricks[3]

young man answered sheepishly, "No. I guess I was working too hard to take the time."[2] The demands of family require large power reserves. If we do not take the time to "sharpen" our lives, our self-generated energy will be quickly depleted, causing burnout. Diligence in training our children begins with how we handle God's Word.

When we give priority to deepening our relationship with God, we will be equipped to become effective workmen.

A Divine Appointment
Read Psalm 34:1-8 and Acts 3:19 in your Bible.
Scripture gives example after example of the need to set time aside to be alone with God. In gardening terms, a divine appointment is like preparing the soil. When we take the time to cultivate our inner world, God will produce great fruit from "average garden variety" parents. It is not just checking off a devotion time that brings the growth, but creating an environment where God can speak, instruct, and build our character. Just as you would set up a time and place to meet someone you want to know better, you may need to take your calendar and literally schedule a "divine appointment" with God. Those who have tasted the difference that sitting with the Lord over a cup of hot chocolate brings to parenting will quickly rearrange their schedules to accommodate daily times of refreshing.

⚙**List three things that currently interfere with regular divine appointments with God. Beside each one, indicate how these obstacles can be removed.**

1. _____

2. _____

3. _____

God's Schedule Is Open for Listening and Speaking
Read Psalm 5:3; Psalm 32:8; 45:1; 57:2; and 143:8 in your Bible.
God anticipates the cries of our hearts and responds to us gladly. God confirms His involvement as our counselor and guide in both small and large details. It doesn't matter so much

when, where, or how structured you are, but consistent communication is the key to deepening any intimate relationship. Not listening is considered pure rudeness, yet stopping to listen to God is the most neglected part of divine appointments. God speaks through His written Word, the Bible. When we read Scripture, then wait quietly, He has the opportunity to instruct, correct, renew, and refresh our tired minds. Close friends allow each other the freedom to share their innermost hopes, fears, doubts, even anger. God invites us to talk to Him honestly and openly through prayer. Prayer has many facets, including praise, thanksgiving, confession, requests, and intercession. One of the most tangible forms of dialogue with God is journaling—simply writing a note or letter to Him. Recording the greatness of who He is (praise), what He has done (thanksgiving), what He has revealed (confession, instruction), and what you and others need (petition, intercession), will be encouraging to look back on and share with your children over the years.

☼**List the ways you spend time with God.**

_____

Based on the ideas presented in this section, what would you add to your list that will draw you closer to God?

_____

The Kids Will Know
Read Isaiah 50:4 and 54:10-14 in your Bible.
Adrian Rogers told of some gold prospectors who discovered an exceptionally rich mine. One of them said, "Hey, we've got it made as long as we don't tell anybody else before we stake our claims." So they each vowed to keep the secret. Because they had to have more tools and provisions, they headed for town. After buying all the supplies they needed, they hurried back to the mine site. But they weren't alone. A crowd of people followed them, because their discovery was written all over their faces.[4] As a disciple of Jesus Christ, you are offered the privilege of sharing in the treasures of God. In a way we cannot comprehend, God can give us His undivided attention. God longs to spend time with you, like your own children long for

Many years ago, there were two men who shared a quality of life that I admired. Both spent time alone with God consistently. Following their example, I began setting aside time in the mornings to memorize Scripture and journal in a notebook. The difference it made in me caused Elaine to take great pains to protect my quiet time, even when she couldn't find as much as she desired. The more God corrected and adjusted my thinking, the more I tried to help her find these times of refreshment. Nothing I have ever done as a dad impacted my parenting like my "divine appointments" with God, and praying for my wife and children every day.—*David*

time alone with you. He knows just what to say to sustain weary moms and dads. God will lead you to rich mines of gold that will make the parenting journey worth continuing, "and the well-being of your sons will be great" (Isaiah 54:13).

Parent Project 3

Part I. Using the illustration on page 38, begin designing your blueprint by becoming a student of each of your children. Work through one of these issues each day this week.

1. Evaluate your child's life and adopt a balanced view of your child's development (Luke 2:52).
2. Observe your child's actions—when they aren't looking (Proverbs 20:11).
3. Join in your child's activities (Romans 12:10).
4. Chronicle your child's milestones (Malachi 3:16).
5. Treasure your child's days (Luke 2:51).

Part II: Begin drafting and implementing your blueprint (big project!).

1. Get away with your spouse, another family member, or a friend for several hours. Allow time to pray together, read Scripture, and complete the following steps.
2. Go back to Parent Talk 3 and look at the compiled character list. Can you think of other qualities to add? Rank the top 10 qualities your child needs and draw them on your blueprint.
3. When and where will you capture teachable moments? Pray for God to give you ideas about teaching each character quality purposefully and creatively. Catalog which books, videos, musical and story tapes you already have. Go through your game shelves and consider which games can be used to teach specific character traits during play.
4. Take each character quality and begin a Scripture study about the quality and persons who did or did not possess those qualities.
5. Establish a personal quiet time to prepare yourself for character building opportunities.

---

[1] Josh McDowell and Bob Hostetler, *Right from Wrong* (Dallas: Word, 1994), 81.
[2] Kent and Barbara Hughes, *Liberating Ministry from the Success Syndrome* (Wheaton: Tyndale House, 1988), 71.
[3] Howard Hendricks, Januray 1991, speaking at the National Network of Youth Ministries National Forum in Glen Erie, Colorado.
[4] Charles Swindoll, *You and Your Child* (Nashville: Thomas Nelson, Bantam Edition, 1980), 8.

Chapter 4
The Discipline Game:
The Object of the Game

PARENT VIEW 4

The most reliable source on discipline is the Word of God. It contains over 200 verses that speak to parents and children.

⌂ Key Principle 1

Discipline means _____.

Teaching deals with the _____, training deals with

the _____. In training we help children

_____ what we have _____ them.

⌂ Key Principle 2

Discipline is a _____, not a _____.

⌂ Key Principle 3

Discipline requires _____, _____

parents.

Golden Rule of Parenting

I can't _____ what I don't have.

⚔ Key Principle 4

The real _____ of discipline is to develop a

_____ and _____ of obedience.

Obedience is _____ _____ the

_____ and _____ of another person.

The Model of Abraham

• He obeyed _____.

• He obeyed without _____ or _____.

• He obeyed _____.

Building Blocks of Obedience

• Age 1-5   _____

• Age 6-12   _____

• Age 13-18   _____

DISCIPLINE IS ...	NOT ...
Training	Teaching only
A tool	A weapon
Instruction and correction	Punishment or correction only
A shaper of character	A manipulator of performance

Parent Talk 4

Use the following as a guide to talk with your spouse, another parent, or group of parents. Pray together as you begin your discussion.

1. Why is discipline such a controversial subject?

2. Give an example of how you have used discipline as a weapon. Give an example of how you have used discipline as a tool.

3. How has The Golden Rule of Parenting—"You cannot transfer what you do not have"—been true in your experience as a parent (or child)?

4. How would you respond to the parent who says, "I love my child too much to punish him"?

5. Read out loud "Drill Sergeant" by Sharon Moss. Discuss what happens when discipline includes only correction. What phrases do you use?

> Clean your room, Pick up your clothes,
> Brush your teeth, and Blow your nose.
> Walk the dog, Feed the cat,
> Don't forget to wear your hat.
>
> Look at you, another spill!
> Wipe it up, And then sit still.
> Watch your tone as you talk to me!
> Say what you want, Just don't disagree.
>
> Shut the door, And do it right,
> Or you'll be in your room all night!
> I've told you hitting will not do.
> If I see it again, Then I'll spank you.
>
> Now take a bath, It's time for bed,
> Let's hurry up, Get those prayers said.
> Tomorrow is church, We can't be late,
> Our parenting class just will not wait.
>
> Now shut your eyes, So we'll have some peace.
> You know we love you, Now get some sleep.[1]

Parent Shaper 4

···

Discipline is vital in the character development of our children. Because it is so important, we have devoted three sessions to this topic. Most of us limit the term *discipline* to mean punishment when, in fact, it is much more. Discipline is a long-term investment requiring a sacrifice of time and energy, but "it produces a harvest of righteousness and peace for those who have been trained by it" (Hebrews 12:11, NIV).

Defining Discipline

Read Proverbs 12:1 and Proverbs 29:17.

If you want to participate in a linguistic spaghetti bowl, try a study of the word *discipline*! Words like *teaching, instruction, training, reproof, rebuke, chastening, chastisement* and *punishment* crisscross throughout the various translations of the Bible. In the verses above, the *New American Standard Bible* uses *discipline* to mean instruction, while the *New International Version* uses it to mean correction. In the *King James Version, discipline* is used only one time in the entire Bible! In the following exercise we will define some of the terms we will encounter in our study on discipline.

⚙**Read the following verses in at least two translations and compare the terms used. Write a brief definition in the margin for each term.**

Instruction: Proverbs 1:8; 4:1-2; and 9:9 (tutoring, education, nurture, training).

Correction: Hebrews 12:9; Proverbs 15:10 (reforming, rectifying, restoring to uprightness, improving life and character).

Reproof: Proverbs 3:11; 6:23; and 15:31-32 (conviction, evidence, testing, discovery).

*Whoever loves discipline
loves knowledge,
But he who hates reproof
is stupid (Proverbs 12:1).*

*Correct your son, and he will
give you comfort;
He will also delight your soul
(Proverbs 29:17).*

TERMS TO DEFINE:

Instruction: _____

_____

Correction: _____

_____

Reproof: _____

_____

43

Rebuke: Proverbs 13:1 and 17:10 (dispute, reason, convince, justify, chide).

Punish: Proverbs 19:19 and 21:11 (to inflict a penalty or fine, condemn).

Chasten—Psalm 94:12; Proverbs 13:24; and Deuteronomy 8:5 (instruction with blows or words; to make tired or disgusted of; to warn, restrain, or check).

Write your definition of discipline.

_____

_____

Discipline Means Training
Read Proverbs 22:6.
Proverbs 22:6 is to parenting what John 3:16 is to evangelism. The principles contained in this one verse form a good foundation on which to build.

Train—The original word in Hebrew is the same term used for "the palate, the roof of the mouth, the gums." In the verb form, *train* is the same term used for breaking a wild horse and bringing it into submission by using a rope in its mouth. The word is also used to describe "developing a thirst" as the midwife massaged the gums of a newborn with date juice to get the baby to begin nursing. The word evolved to mean "dedicate" or "consecrate." When we say *train*, we usually think of teaching, but training is more than teaching.

Child—Most of us would define a child as under age 12, but *child* is used throughout the Old Testament to cover every stage from infancy to adulthood. The period of training continues until our children leave home to live on their own!

In—This little word means "in keeping with, in cooperation with, or according to."

The way he should go—Literally, *way* means how the child is bent. Each child is born with a unique personality and traits that "give" naturally in one direction more easily than another. Chuck Swindoll says it well in *You and Your Child*: "In every child God places in our arms, there is a *bent*, a set of

TERMS TO DEFINE (CONT.):

Rebuke: _____

_____

Punish: _____

_____

Chasten: _____

_____

Train a child in the way he should go, and when he is old he will not turn from it (Proverbs 22:6, NIV).

I have a job to do that isn't that complicated, but is often very difficult—to get a group of men to do what they don't want to do so they can achieve what they've wanted all their lives
—Tom Landry, former coach of the Dallas Cowboys[2]

characteristics already established. The bent is fixed and determined before he is given over to our care. The child is not, in fact, a pliable piece of clay. He has been set; he has been bent. And the parents who want to train their child correctly will discover that bent."[3] Some children are trained best by explanation. Others must learn by experience. Some cry if you look at them sideways. Some are motivated by a challenge, while others are only moved by a threat. We will find less resistance when we learn the approach to training that best suits each child. *His* best way may not be *your* best way—and it may be different for each child you have!

When he is old he will not depart from it—Many use this verse to encourage parents of prodigals that as adults—or at least before death—their children will return to the Lord if their training was good. Some contend that all children automatically turn away from parents' teachings during adolescence. Indeed there are diligent parents whose children make ungodly choices. *Old* actually means "bearded one" as well has "hair on the chin." Our success will become evident as early as the "peach fuzz" years. A teenager can and will walk in the ways he has learned and practiced the first 12 years. But parents can't expect much if they miss opportunities to train. This news is both exciting and terrifying to those who believe there is still plenty of time to start. Pursue excellence today to avoid regrets tomorrow!

Rewrite Proverbs 22:6 in your own words.

_____

_____

Discipline Demonstrates Love
Read 1 Samuel 2—3 in your Bible.
Some parents say, "I love my children too much to punish them." Unwittingly, these parents have been deceived. Hebrews 12:6 says, "The Lord disciplines those He loves" (NIV). Eli was a father who had a similar attitude toward discipline. Though he had some admirable traits, he tended to scrutinize the behavior of others rather than pay attention to his own family. Eli's two grown sons were described as wicked men with no regard for the Lord (1 Samuel 2:12). While Eli was perched outside the

---

Discipline is like baking a cake—you don't realize you have a disaster until it is too late!!—James Dobson[4]

Inside Look
When I was six, just before we were leaving for a family vacation, I stole a huge amount of change from my mother and hid it in a can under the back porch steps. When we got in the car, my mother gave us each a new little wallet and told us she had saved money so we could have a little to spend each day of the trip. When she reached into her purse to pull the money out, it was gone. I never told her what I had done, but God knew—and when I went back to get the money from the can, it was gone!—*David*

It is harder to lead a family than to rule a nation—Chinese Proverb[6]

Youngsters . . . get more information by observing those persons who are close to them. Children tend to value what they see their parents valuing. If there happens to be consistency between what the parents *say* they value and what they *show*, this value will become strong in the life of the child. If there is no consistency, the child will become even more confused.—Earl D. Wilson, *Try Being a Teenager!*[6]

temple, his sons spent their time misleading and cheating worshippers. Everyone in Israel knew it—except Eli. Instead of taking action, he merely said, "Why do you do such things?" (2:23, NIV). Nothing changed until God took control and pronounced their impending doom. Eli's sin was defined: You "honor your sons more than me" (2:29, NIV). In the end, the sins of the sons and the passivity of their father affected their family, their community, and the entire nation of Israel. It may seem overdramatic to say America will be affected if we do not discipline our children, but consider the upbringing of the generation who now leads our country—and what about the generation of young people we read about every day? Is the stretch really all that far?

A Biblical Model for Discipline
Read Genesis 22:1-14 in your Bible.
So how do you do discipline? You cannot transfer what you do not have. One father who modeled the kind of obedience we desire was Abraham. Like many parents, Abraham had learned to obey God the hard way. Once he did learn, he was able to transfer that same pattern of obedience to his son.

Immediately—When God told him to sacrifice his child, whose birth in itself was a miracle, he obeyed without hesitation.

Without question or complaint—Abraham believed God's promises were good and had learned God knows what He is doing even when we don't.

Completely—When God gave specific instructions, Abraham carried them out to the letter. Abraham had learned that God's plan is the only plan.

☼**As a parent, how do you measure up in your obedience to God? Circle the area that is most difficult for you. Ask God to help you in this area.**

The obedience transferred to his son outweighs Abraham's pattern of obedience. After all, Isaac was the one being sacrificed. Genesis 22:6-9 shows how Isaac demonstrated the same characteristics of his father. He was probably strong enough to physically resist the aging Abraham, but he allowed his father to bind him on the altar. His only question was, "Where is the lamb for the burnt offering?" (22:7). When Abraham assured him, he obeyed without another word. God honored the obedience of the father and son. What a demonstration of discipline by example!

Few of our children's peers will be required to obey in this manner, but this is a worthy aim in all we pursue. Learning to obey *immediately* may save your child's life one day. Obedience *without question or complaint* will establish positive attitudes that will aid in relating to authority throughout life. *Complete* obedience will avoid any regrets.

You Cannot Transfer What You Do Not Have (and You Will Transfer What You Do Have)

Read Matthew 15:1-9 and Titus 1:16 in your Bible.

The Pharisees and religious leaders couldn't fool Jesus, even though they led many others to believe they were spiritual giants. Parents, one place you can't fool others is in your own home! You may pull the wool over your toddler's eyes, but eventually she will see you for who you are. One of the rites of passage from boyhood to manhood is the first shave. One dad's two-year-old son wandered into the bathroom just as he started to shave. He studied what his father was doing, noticed the little brush in the razor case and began shaving—just like his father. When Dad shaved his right cheek, Joseph shaved his. He cocked his head the same way and squinted his eyes the same way. He didn't miss a motion. That imitation goes beyond just mimicking a shave, doesn't it? Our little guys look to us for the many facets of manhood. We are their models. I try to remember that principle often—like every time I shave.[7]

⚙**What character qualities do you see in your children that reflect who you are? List them in the margin.**

Start with the Small Things

Read Colossians 3:20 and Luke 16:10.

Parents today have a tendency to worry ahead of time about "big" things like drugs, pregnancy, and AIDS to the exclusion of "smaller" things like manners, hard work, and respectful responses. These verses provide an important principle for developing obedience in everything—start with little things! If we hope to see the day when our kids will come home from their dates on time or resist cheating even when "everyone else

CHARACTER QUALITIES
TRANSFERRED FROM
ME TO MY CHILDREN

_____

_____

_____

_____

_____

_____

Children, be obedient to your parents in all things, for this is well-pleasing to the Lord (Colossians 3:20).

"He who is faithful in a very little thing is faithful also in much; and he who is unrighteous in a very little thing is unrighteous also in much" (Luke 16:10).

47

♥Inside Look

I remember being an obedient child for the most part. But for some reason, my parents didn't break me of "sassing" and arguing with them. I do remember them saying, "You'd argue with a bull in a china cabinet!" I still struggle with my mouth as an adult. We have one child in particular to whom that lovely pattern has been transferred. Because I haven't quite finished my own discipline process, we can both go several rounds in the proverbial china cabinet. God must get frustrated having to simultaneously train the teacher and the student!
—*Elaine*

is doing it," we must establish obedience in related areas when they are young. Respect for teachers and other authority figures starts with the toddler being taught to say yes (instead of *uh-huh*), please, and thank you. In this week's video segment, we introduced the illustration of the building blocks for discipline. During the years from 13 to 18, children who have learned to do right (by action), and to do right consistently (by habit and principle), are better prepared to do right by choice (character). Even teens prone to experimenting or rebelling during this time are more likely to respond appropriately if the other building blocks have been carefully laid.

☼**What small things do you need to work on with your children? List two or three in the first column. What issues do you need to go back a step to "retrain" as actions or habits? List them in the second column.**

_____   _____

_____   _____

_____   _____

Discipline Draws Hearts
Read Acts 2:38-41 and 1 Timothy 4:7-10 in your Bible.
Peter challenged parents to personally receive and identify with the gospel, then extended the promise to future generations (Acts 2:39). Timothy challenged us to discipline ourselves since godliness is profitable now and later. He weighs bodily discipline against spiritual discipline and godliness wins hands down. God uses believing, disciplined parents to draw children to Himself. When our boys were almost seven, my journal entry read, "Blake and Joel seem sensitive to sin and near to giving You their hearts. Understanding that key concept that they need you for life itself is my prayer. Help me to display that You are my Banner—my salvation, my protection and power. As Amanda [age four] takes it all in, begin preparing her heart to receive you." As children learn to distinguish right from wrong, they begin to grasp the concept of sin and its consequences. Parents can begin telling their children at an early age about God's wonderful purpose for their lives and that learning to

obey now will prepare them for His calling later.

☼**How have you communicated the principle of a "special calling" to your children?**

_____

_____

The Rewards of Discipline

Read Hebrews 12:5-11 and 1 John 3:2 in your Bible.

A man found a cocoon containing an emperor moth, and took it home to watch it [a rare butterfly] emerge. One day a small opening appeared, and for several hours the moth struggled but couldn't seem to force its body past a certain point. Deciding something was wrong, the man took scissors and snipped the remaining bit of cocoon. The moth emerged easily, its body large and swollen, the wings small and shriveled. He expected that in a few hours the wings would spread out in their natural beauty, but they did not. Instead of developing into a creature free to fly, the moth spent its life dragging around a swollen body and shriveled wings. The constricting cocoon and the struggle necessary to pass through the tiny opening are the Creator's way of forcing fluid from the body into the wings. The "merciful" snip was, in reality, cruel.[8]

God deals with you as with sons; for what son is there whom his father does not discipline? ... All discipline for the moment seems not to be joyful, but sorrowful; yet to those who have been trained by it, afterwards it yields the peaceful fruit of righteousness (Hebrews 12:7,11).

Instructing and correcting your children will present struggles for them and for you. There will be times when it feels like you are hindering them, when you are ultimately setting them free to "fly" during adulthood. Having righteous children who are at peace with God and others sounds like fruit worth cultivating. And someday, somehow, all of us will look like Jesus!

☼**Spend time praying for your child and yourself, remembering to thank God for both the struggle and the rewards to come.**

49

Parent Project 4

On a separate sheet of paper, use the following strategy to systematically work through a discipline issue with your child.

DISCIPLINE STRATEGY
James 1:5, 3:17-18

1. Describe the problem or challenge in detail. My child …

2. This issue concerns (list all that apply) …
   - Respect
   - Responsibility
   - Action
   - Attitude
   - Other …
   - Immediate obedience
   - Obedience without question
   - Obedience without complaint
   - Complete obedience

3. The child's intent seems to be …

4. The instruction I have given is …

5. The correction I have given is …

6. I am trying to train my child to (put in positive terms) …

7. The character quality I am focusing on is …

---

[1] Sharon Moss, "Drill Sargeant." Used by permission of the author.
[2] Tim Kimmel, *Legacy of Love* (Portland: Multnomah, 1989), 108.
[3] Charles Swindoll, *You and Your Child* (New York: Bantam, 1984), 9.
[4] James Dobson, *Focus on the Family* radio program.
[5] Steve Farrar, *Point Man* (Portland: Multnomah, 1990), 11.
[6] Earl D. Wilson, *Try Being a Teenager* (Portland, OR: Multnomah Press, 1982), 114.
[7] *Pulpit Helps*, October 1991, 20.
[8] Billy Beacham, *Growing in Godliness Leader's Guide* (Fort Worth: Student Discipleship Ministries, 1986), 13-14.

Chapter 5
The Discipline Game: Playing the Game

PARENT VIEW 5

Discipline is like a two-sided coin: on one side is instruction and on the other side is correction. We must balance both.

SCRIPTURE USED DURING THE VIDEO SESSION ...
Colossians 3:20
Ecclesiastes 4:9
Galatians 6:9

⚘ Key Principle 1

Prescribe age-appropriate _____ _____ for

each child.

Examples:

Character Goals ⟶ _____

Behavior Goals ⟶ _____

Once the goal is identified, we need to establish

_____ and _____.

Guideline Examples

• _____ your opponent when you lose.

• _____ your opponent when you win.

Boundary Examples

• Do not lose your _____ over a loss.

• Do not _____ or _____-_____ over a victory.

Central Question: What am I trying to _____?

⌂ Key Principle 2

Behavior goals should balance _____ and _____.

Respect: preference, _____, admiration, and

_____

Responsibility: reliability, _____, and trustworthiness

Is what I'm trying to train an issue of respect or responsibility?

Have I considered both _____ and _____?

⌂ Key Principle 3

Establish your family's _____ and _____.

Developing Your Discipline Plan

1. Set behavior goals, guidelines, and boundaries _____.

2. Determine guidelines and boundaries _____ they are needed.

3. Guidelines and boundaries must be _____

_____.

4. The _____ behind the guidelines and boundaries should be _____.

⌂ Key Principle 4

Always respond to both _____ and

_____.

Parent Talk 5

Use the following as a guide to talk with your spouse, another parent, or group of parents. Pray together as you begin your discussion.

1. What are the benefits of setting specific discipline goals?

2. Which area of training is your strongest: respect or responsibility? Why do you feel that way?

3. Share an example of a time when it was beneficial to have guidelines and boundaries established before they were needed. How did it benefit you? your child?

4. With which age range of children do you find it most difficult to communicate? What can you do to become a better communicator with this group?

5. Share specific ways you are shaping your child's attitude. … influencing your child's actions.

6. Why is it important to provide a consequence for both obedience and disobedience?

7. What are some ways you discern your child's intent?

You shall rise up before the grayheaded, and honor the aged, and you shall revere your God; I am the Lord (Leviticus 19:32).

He must be one who manages his own household well, keeping his children under control with all dignity (1 Timothy 3:4).

Like apples of gold in settings of silver
Is a word spoken in right circumstances
(Proverbs 25:11).

Be devoted to one another in brotherly love; give preference to one another in honor (Romans 12:10).

Parent Shaper 5

....

he discipline game not only involves our understanding the object of the game; we must also play the game (as we will see in this chapter), and play to win (chapter 6).

Goals for Respect
Read Leviticus 19:32; 1 Timothy 3:4; and Proverbs 25:11.
Are you honored in your own home? Our beginning point for setting proper discipline goals is to identify which targets are appropriate for the child's stage of physical, intellectual, social, and spiritual development. Once you have designed your character blueprint (p. 38), you can use each quality to set short-term training goals. In session 6 you will learn strategies and tools to help you reach those goals. Most discipline goals fall into the categories of respect and responsibility. In *How to Raise Your Children for Christ*, Andrew Murray says the fifth commandment (Exodus 20:12) is pivotal to those before and after it. The first four commandments deal with our relationship to God; the final five deal with our relationship to people. Sandwiched between the two groups is the fifth commandment, "Honor your father and your mother." Leviticus 19:32 demonstrates that honoring parents has been an age-old problem. Children who do not honor their parents will not honor God or others later.[1]

☼**How is Romans 12:10 being modeled in your home?**

_____

_____

Goals for Responsibility
Read Proverbs 27:18; Romans 14:12; and Proverbs 6:6-8 in your Bible.
Part of showing respect for God, parents, and others is learning

54

The Discipline Game: Playing the Game

responsibility for ourselves. When our children grow up, they will be accountable for their actions the same way we are. Training in responsibility is essential for independence. Neglecting or postponing this training actually handicaps our children's growth. There are many lessons found in nature that help teach this important principle.

> *Four things are small on the earth,*
> *But they are exceedingly wise:*
> *The ants are not a strong folk,*
> *But they prepare their food in the summer;*
> *The badgers are not mighty folk,*
> *Yet they make their houses in the rocks;*
> *The locusts have no king,*
> *Yet all of them go out in ranks;*
> *The lizard you may grasp with the hands,*
> *Yet it is in kings' palaces (Proverbs 30:24-28).*

Young children want to feel "big" and early responsibility gives them both power and independence!

List areas of responsibility your child can participate in at his present age.

_____

_____

How are you balancing goals for respect and responsibility?

_____

_____

Consider Both Action and Attitude
Read 1 Samuel 2:3 and Psalm 131:1-2 in your Bible.
Some parents set rules and guidelines for outward behavior without considering the attitude with which their child obeys. The child sitting in time-out on a little chair in the corner said to her doll, "I'm sittin' down on the outside, but I'm standin' up on

Inside Look
Because our children are close in age, we have observed how differently they react within a similar environment. All three have unique character strengths and flaws that emerged during the preschool years and have stayed basically the same. It is especially fascinating to me that Joel and Blake are identical twins—one half of the same egg, sharing all the same genes and chromosomes—yet from day one they have been as individually wired as any two human beings. Amanda demonstrates positive actions and attitudes we haven't ever had to work at, and struggles with other attitudes that the boys are rarely corrected for.—*David*

55

O Lord, my heart is not proud, nor my eyes haughty;
Nor do I involve myself in great matters,
Or in things too difficult for me.
Surely I have composed and quieted my soul;
Like a weaned child rests against his mother,
My soul is like a weaned child within me.
O Israel, hope in the Lord From this time forth and forever (Psalm 131).

Two are better than one because they have a good return for their labor. For if either of them falls, the one will lift up his companion. But woe to the one who falls when there is not another to lift him up (Ecclesiastes 4:9-10).

Without consultation, plans are frustrated, But with many counselors they succeed (Proverbs 15:22).

the inside!" By the age of three or four, the attitude component has presented itself. As Matthew 6:22 puts it, the eyes are a lamp to the soul. "Haughty" eyes are one of six things God hates (Proverbs 6:17). Signs of disobedience in attitude include a sour face, "poochy" lips, sassing, arguing, negotiating, sulking, eye-rolling, and throwing a tantrum. Remember that obedience without question or complaint is an important part of complete obedience.

☼**Which signs of disobedience in attitude listed above are patterns in your child? Circle them.**
… in yourself? Underline them. Read Psalm 131 and adopt it as a character goal for you and your children.

Determine Together Guidelines and Boundaries
Read Ecclesiastes 4:9-10 and Proverbs 15:22.
One of the worst things that can happen to a child is to receive mixed signals about what is appropriate and inappropriate. Disagreements about discipline are common. Depending on each spouse's background and temperament, a variety of issues emerge. Two-parent families as well as single-parent families with shared custody should take pains to come to an agreement on standard house rules. A single parent should seek counsel and accountability from other adults involved in the care of the child or with a small group of parents working together. When you meet periodically to discuss training goals, you will develop purpose and confidence knowing you are on a team executing the same game plan.

☼**What is your greatest obstacle to presenting a secure, united front for your child? What will you do to remove this obstacle?**

_____

_____

Set Guidelines and Boundaries Before They Are Needed
Read 2 Timothy 4:2 and Proverbs 16:3 in your Bible.
We will never think of every situation, but we can identify quite a few common to all children. If we wait to establish bound-aries, we are more likely to let the emotion of the moment drive

our response. Someone will flush, eat, or spill something horrible at some point and we will overreact. Setting realistic, practical guidelines takes some ingenuity: "We keep the lid on our cup." "We hold a cup with both hands." "We keep the cup on the red circle." There will always be unpredictable disasters like the one our former baby-sitter encountered. When our boys were 10, a college girl kept them on the days I (Elaine) worked. At the beginning of the summer, I gave her a list of family rules so she would be prepared. She worried that so many rules would make them dislike her, so she ignored them. One day, the boys locked her inside the swimming pool gate for a couple of hours (a neighbor rescued her). I'll have to admit that was one situation I wasn't prepared for! I made them lie down for about three hours until I could get in touch with David and figure out how to respond.

☼**Do you tend to act or react to situations that come up in your home? Considering your child's age, what are some common issues you can plan for?**

_____

_____

According to Proverbs 16:3, what promise does God give prepared parents? Underline it in the margin.

Communicate Guidelines Clearly
Read Ecclesiastes 12:9-11 and Romans 15:14 in your Bible.
In *Point Man*, Steve Farrar shared a story told by David Roper. His family was at a conference center, and he and his wife were seated with the conference director in the lodge. Right behind the lodge was a recently seeded embankment with signs that said, *KEEP OFF THE BANK*. Suddenly the conference director jumped up and shouted, "Stay off the bank!" and ran out the door. To Roper's horror, there was one of his boys poised right at the top of the bank. Mortified, his father took him around the building, got a little switch and kept saying, "Son, didn't you hear that man say 'Stay off the bank?' " As they walked back, the little boy looked up with tear-stained eyes and asked, "Daddy, what's a bank?"[2] Parents may establish rules easily

Commit your works to the Lord, And your plans will be established (Proverbs 16:3).

♥Inside Look
When we had twins, people often commented that we had been "doubly blessed." When Amanda turned out to be a quiet little girl, we were delighted, because the boys had become "double trouble"! They climbed on the refrigerator, pulled wires out of the air conditioner, and flushed contact lenses down the toilet. One time, the toilets in our home had to be removed from the floor because of all the toys that would not go down. A decade later, not much has changed!
—*David and Elaine*

❦**Inside Look**
In fifth grade, Amanda was asked to write a paragraph about a "Goliath" in her own life. Her teacher thought we should save what she wrote: "My brothers, Blake and Joel are like Goliath to me today, because we just get mad, argue, and hurt each other. My brothers pick on me like little scabs on their arms. They really hurt my feelings, I've learned how to handle my problems with them."
—*Elaine*

And this is love, that we walk according to His commandments. This is the commandment, just as you have heard from the beginning, that you should walk in it (2 John 6).

I have no greater joy that to hear that my children are walking in the truth (3 John 4).

enough, but they must be communicated meaningfully on the child's language level before expecting obedience. The secret is patience and persistence. We must make it simple enough for two year olds with basic statements like "Make your feet stop" or "Toys go in the basket." Once we figure out how to translate our wishes into "childrenese" we must repeat them many times to establish understanding. You will have to test and retest, explaining new concepts, then asking, "What did Mom say?" or "What is the rule about …?" until it gets settled in their minds. Later you will begin to discern when disobedience is from honest confusion or feigned ignorance!

☼**How do you determine when your children understand what you want them to do? When does a rule become enforceable at your house?**

_____

_____

Explain the Purpose for Guidelines
Read 2 John 6 and 3 John 4.
Even though very young children may not pick up all the meaning, it is never too soon to explain why you set certain boundaries. When you tell your child to stay on the driveway, you can add, "This is our rule because I want you to be safe." Kids resent the attitude of "Just because I said so"; but there are times when it will be appropriate to say, "God has made me responsible for you and I have a bad feeling about that." Children who recognize that our motivation is love and concern generally want to comply with our wishes. Remember the building blocks of action, habit, and character? The habit stage (ages 6 to 12) is a critical period for passing on the logical and biblical principles that will help them choose to do right on their own. Sharing Scripture to back up discipline also confirms that our aims are God's will.

☼**Do you explain to your children why you set certain boundaries? Monitor what you say as you discipline your children today.**

Determine If It Is Ignorance, Immaturity, or Rebellion

Read Psalm 78:8; Acts 17:30; and 1 Corinthians 13:11 in your Bible.

There have been horrifying news stories about parents who harmed or even killed infants who wouldn't stop crying or toddlers who broke something valuable. Parents of young children must ask themselves a vital question before responding to negative behavior or disobedience: Was it childish irresponsibility or willful disobedience? How we respond to ignorance or immaturity is different from our response to direct, willful disobedience. The aim is to adjust our consequences to the child's intent. A 7 month old exploring a plug is ignorance. A 10 month old pulling a full pitcher out of the refrigerator is immaturity. A 2 year old making waves overflow from the tub is irresponsibility. A 4 year old touching a hot light bulb is ignorance. A 6 year old splashing in a puddle in new shoes is immaturity. An 8 year old losing a library book is irresponsibility. In most cases, these children need instruction. The exception would be if the child is motivated by power, revenge, or defiance. New parents will quickly learn to recognize the gleam in the eye that distinguishes between the two. Usually between 8 and 18 months, parents will identify the look that communicates, "I know exactly what you're saying and I'm gonna do it my way."

✲ **How do you typically respond to things your child does that demonstrate …**

ignorance? _____

immaturity? _____

rebellion? _____

Respond to Obedience and Disobedience

Read Galatians 6:7-9.

There is a law of sowing which can't be denied—When you plant seeds, they produce a harvest. If you don't plant, you don't reap. If you plant pumpkins, you don't get watermelons. The harvest is the evidence of what was planted. This illustration is

Do not be deceived, God is not mocked; for whatever a man sows, this he will also reap. For the one who sows to his own flesh shall from the flesh reap corruption, but the one who sows to the Spirit shall from the Spirit reap eternal life. And let us not lose heart in doing good, for in due time we shall reap if we do not grow weary (Galatians 6:7-9).

❦Inside Look

During the first week of sixth grade, the boys were getting used to having male teachers for the first time. On the first day, the science teacher told the class to be sitting quietly with their books ready when he walked into the room. The next day, he came into class and asked anyone who had been talking before he arrived to join him in the hall. Joel was one of several who came forward for punishment (according to him, there were several more who did not). When they got outside, the teacher handed each one a Gold Homework Pass and congratulated them for showing so much integrity. Joel's reaction was, "Man! That really makes me want to do the right thing!"
—*David*

often used to warn about bad behavior, but sometimes we forget that the sowing principle works both ways. There should always be a consequence whether the child responds in disobedience or obedience. Consequences teach the child that every action and attitude matter to you and to God. If there is no consequence after disobedience, children eventually learn that sin has no price. If there is no consequence for obedience, children eventually become discouraged about the futility of trying to please God. Parents often wait to respond until a child disobeys. Try to catch them behaving, then respond so they don't "lose heart" and "grow weary" of doing right. Many times the harvest they hope to reap is your attention and if sowing disobedience gets the job done, a large crop of disobedience will be harvested! When we are careful to notice and praise our child's good actions, words, and attitudes, they will become more motivated to sow seeds of goodness and kindness.

☼**Most parents can readily identify how they respond to their child's disobedience. How do you respond when your child obeys you immediately or without being asked?**

_____

_____

Close your study in prayer. Ask God to direct you in the way you discipline your children.

Parent Project 5

1. Take this discipline check-up. Circle the word that best describes your current approach to discipline.

   My approach to discipline is usually **offensive / defensive**.
   My responses are usually **consistent / inconsistent**.
   The front generally presented to the children is **unity / disharmony**.
   My child is probably feeling a sense of **security / insecurity** because of my approach to discipline.

   In order to be more effective in discipline, I will:

   _____

2. Establish a regular time with your spouse or friend to set goals and evaluate your discipline plan.

3. Begin the tradition of the family meeting—a regularly scheduled time when all family members make plans for family jobs and fun, express concerns, resolve conflicts, and make decisions. Family meetings give everyone the opportunity to be heard. This is a time to recognize the good things happening in the family and to encourage each other. Focus on what the family can do to resolve conflicts. Each family meeting should include plans for recreation or other special activities. Behavior contracts can also be established and negotiated.

[1] Andrew Murray, *How to Raise Your Children for Christ* (Minneapolis: Bethany House, 1975), 81.
[2] Steve Farrar, *Point Man* (Portland: Multnomah, 1990), 259-60.

Chapter 6
The Discipline Game: Playing to Win

SCRIPTURE USED DURING THE VIDEO SESSION ...
Proverbs 23:15-16
Proverbs 22:15
Proverbs 29:15
2 Corinthians 7:10

PARENT VIEW 6

There is a great reward for discipline—we'll be able to see our children develop a thirst for obedience and our hearts will be encouraged.

⚠ Key Principle 1

Use _____-_____ tools of discipline to

reinforce _____.

Tools That Reinforce Obedience

1 Praise the _____ of the child.

2. Affirm the _____ of the child.

3. Use _____ rewards.

4. Use _____ rewards.

⚠ Key Principle 2

Use _____-_____ tools of discipline to correct

_____.

Tools That Correct Disobedience

1. Spanking

2. Natural and _____ consequences

3. _____ appropriate behavior

4. Time-out / _____

5. _____ assistance

6. Remove _____ privileges.

⌂ Key Principle 3

We must _____ the _____ of

our discipline.

Key Questions

1. What did I _____?

2. Did I _____ my child?

3. Was there _____ or _____?

4. Is my child's _____ open?

Parent Talk 6

Use the following as a guide to talk with your spouse, another parent, or group of parents. Pray together as you begin your discussion.

1. Respond to the statement: Rules without relationship result in rebellion.

2. Evaluate tools you use for obedience and disobedience. Select one and use the following questions to talk about it.
   - Is this tool age-appropriate for my child?
   - What does this tool train? How does it instruct or correct?
   - What are some examples of situations where this tool makes sense?
   - Have I been using this tool properly? consistently?
   - How effective is this tool for training my child?
   - What changes do I need to make to use the tool wisely?

3. Which tool of discipline presented in the video segment was new to you? Which tool do you use that was not mentioned?

4. How often do you use a specific tool after obedience? Which tool(s) for obedience do you think you should try or exercise more consistently?

5. Which of the following reaction traps do you fall into most often: reminding, coaxing, threatening, or excusing? What can you do to avoid this trap?

6. Name some situations where you can give your child the freedom to select between two or more appropriate choices.

Parent Shaper 6

In disciplining our children, there are objectives we want to achieve. We want to encourage rather than discourage. We want our children to understand the difference between who they are and what they do. We want to show our pleasure in their good behavior, while encouraging good responses in the future. Let's look at some tools that will help us achieve these objectives with our children.

BUILD AND REINFORCE OBEDIENCE

1. Praise performance
Read Proverbs 27:2.
Like a drill sergeant points out every minute error made by his squad, or the border patrol waits for an illegal alien to cross the line, some parents wait for a child to make one wrong move. If you want to encourage a child to obey, praise her when she does! This moves discipline from a defensive to an offensive mode. Examples: "I like the way you obeyed the first time" or, "I'm proud of how you have been sharing with your sister," or, "Your kind voice is as warm as sunshine!"

2. Affirm personhood
Read Proverbs 23:15-16.
Our children must know that their identity and our acceptance are not based on their performance. Affirmation is different than praise because it focuses on the person rather than performance alone. "I love your sweet spirit" or "You really showed courage today," leave a strong impression about the child's value to her parents and to God. We should avoid phrases such as, "You are a bad girl" or "You're a liar" because God doesn't base our identity or His acceptance on our performance. Although God hates sin (performance), He loves His children (personhood).

♥Inside Look
Amanda was having problems with tantrums when things didn't go her way. One of the things she wanted was a new doll. To motivate a good attitude, we made a chart dividing the days into morning, afternoon, and evening. When she made it through the morning without a tantrum, she got to place a happy face in the square. If she "blew up" in the afternoon, no happy face would go up. It took three weeks to achieve five days without a tantrum and get the little doll she had wanted. Over a year later, she remembered that lesson and told me she thought she might need another "attitude chart"!
—*Elaine*

Let another praise you, and not your own mouth;
A stranger, and not your own lips (Proverbs 27:2).

My son, if your heart is wise, My own heart will be glad; And my inmost being will rejoice, When your lips speak what is right (Proverbs 23:15-16).

*The wicked earns
deceptive wages,
But he who sows righteousness gets a true reward
(Proverbs 11:18).*

*The fear of the Lord is
clean, enduring forever;
The judgments of the Lord
are true; they are righteous
altogether.
They are more desirable
than gold, yes, than much
fine gold;
Sweeter also than honey
and the drippings of the
honeycomb.
Moreover, by them Thy
servant is warned;
In keeping them there is
great reward
(Psalm 19:9-11).*

*Correct your son, and he
will give you comfort;
He will also delight
your soul.
Where there is no vision,
the people are unrestrained,
But happy is he who keeps
the law
(Proverbs 29:17-18).*

3. Give tangible rewards

Read Proverbs 11:18.

Tangible rewards can be seen, touched, or eaten: ice cream, homework passes, stickers, toys, tickets, or treats are a few examples. The proper use of these rewards is to express your pleasure after a period of good behavior: "You can get something from the treasure box since you sat so quietly during class." Tangible rewards can be overused and can train conditional obedience: "What will you give me to behave?" "I'll give you gum if you stop screaming," is an improper use of rewards.

4. Give intangible rewards

Read Psalm 19:9-11.

Things as simple as a hug, backrub, story, extra time alone with Dad, or playing a game are intangible ways to reinforce good behavior. For instance, "Let's do something you want to do, since you didn't interrupt while I was on the phone," or "We'll read an extra book since you finished your homework early." Intangible rewards make memories while encouraging good responses.

☼ **Review the four tools just discussed. Circle the one you use most often. Underline the one that is new to you and that you will try with your children.**

CONFRONT AND DISCOURAGE DISOBEDIENCE

Read Proverbs 29:17-18.

A child not restrained or reproved is a disgrace to his family. He or she is also unhappy and unfulfilled because there is no direction or vision for life. Let's look at nine tools to confront and discourage disobedience.

1. Spank with Great Care

Read Proverbs 13:24; 22:15; 23:13-14; 29:15 in your Bible.

Spanking is one of the most misunderstood and misused tools. Some parents believe spanking should never be used. Some think of it as a last resort. Others believe it is the only tool. Even those who believe spanking has a place in the discipline process struggle with the proper time and way to use it. The Bible has more to say about this tool of discipline than any of the others.

A neutral instrument—The Old Testament uses an obsolete Hebrew word *shebet* (shay'bet) which means "to branch off" or literally "a stick." This suggests the use of an instrument like a switch.

A particular person— Spanking is for the child who lacks understanding, will not respond to direction, or demands his own way.

A loving purpose—Spanking is used to give wisdom, to control and keep on the path, to remove or drive foolishness from the heart, and to "save his soul" (Proverbs 23:14).

A serious matter—This tool requires diligence, self-control, and love for the child. S*pare* (Proverbs 13:24) means to "refuse or withhold." Sparing the rod is compared to hating the child and keeping the child's heart bound in sin. In fact, disobedience to parents is listed as a characteristic of falling away from God's truth in the last days (2 Timothy 3:1-2).

Pre-Spanking Checklist

- Never appropriate from 0 to 7 months (no direct punishment, regardless of behavior!).
- Generally not necessary from 8 to 14 months (consistent, persistent distractions and diversions are usually enough).
- Most effective first direct punishment from 15 to 24 months for the child who votes no.
- Less frequently used from 9 to 12 years; rarely used after age 12—because other tools are more effective.
- Use when intent is willful, direct disobedience or defiance.
- Use a switch or wooden spoon (goal: painful memory without permanent marks).
- Predetermine the number of swats and where they will be placed (back of leg or bottom represents turning the back on obedience).
- **If your anger is out of control, don't use this tool!**
- Explain why you are spanking: "I want you to remember that it hurts when you disobey."
- After genuine tears, affirm the child and assure your love.
- Move on with your day—it's over.

---

2. Allow Natural Consequences

Read Proverbs 5:23 on the next page.

Another way to say this is, "Let nature take its course." Natural consequences allow circumstances to evolve in order to train

---

❤Inside Look

We decided the most practical "rod of correction" was a light, wooden spoon or a thin switch from a bush, but we tried a fly swatter and a plastic spatula at other times. Going to get the spanking spoon helped us avoid impulsive actions. When our kids still wore diapers, we placed the swats on the soft, fat spot on the back of the thigh. When there wasn't so much padding, they were applied to the bottom! Part of the discussion included our model for obedience: "Did you obey immediately? without complaint? completely? One swat was received for each issue that applied. If they weren't honest or purposely deceived us, they received an extra swat. The consistent use of this tool made spankings less necessary and frequent. We don't spank anymore, but we do have a commercial-sized plastic spatula named "Big Brother" that serves as a good reminder!—*David*

He will die for lack of discipline, led astray by his own folly (Proverbs 5:23).

He is on the path of life who heeds instruction,
But he who forsakes reproof goes astray
(Proverbs 10:17).

For even when we were with you, we used to give you this order: if anyone will not work, neither let him eat. For we hear that some among you are leading an undisciplined life, doing no work at all (2 Thessalonians 3:10-11).

children to obey. If a child leaves his toy car in the yard after being warned to put it away, leave it in the yard, even if it gets ruined. If you always intervene when they lose their new tennis shoes, forget their homework, or break a neighbor's window, you will be reinforcing irresponsibility or disrespect. Allowing your child to reap what she sows provides an indirect form of correction which you can follow up with direct instruction.

3. Enforce Logical Consequences
Read Proverbs 10:17 and 2 Thessalonians 3:10-11.
We *do not* intervene with natural consequences. With logical consequences, we *do* intervene. At times, natural consequences are too costly. An expensive bicycle left in the rain can "disappear" for a specified period of time. A used "cheat sheet" in your daughter's backpack may need to be turned in to the teacher. This tool, when used consistently, trains children to think before they act and consider the inevitable consequences first.

4. Verbalize Appropriate Behavior
Read Proverbs 4:1-6 and 9:9 in your Bible.
Parents waste energy telling kids what not to do. "Stop yelling." "Get your feet off the couch." Young children don't always know the alternative behaviors to our negative correction. While behaviors like these need correction, it doesn't have to be done in a negative way. Your correction can become a time of instruction. A successful approach is to tell children what they should do. "Use an inside voice." "Your feet go on the floor." Positive statements communicate the behavior you are looking for and sound much nicer. It works well with spouses, too!

5. Discuss, Explain, Command, Warn (Once!)
Read Proverbs 16:22 and 23:23 in your Bible.
When he was three, Blake hit his baby sister as he swung his toy lawn mower in the air. I explained that the mower belonged on the grass and Amanda could get seriously hurt if he swung it again. I reminded him of the stitches he got once when a toy hit his head. He remembered for awhile, but started swinging it again (not in defiance) so I moved to a command, "Keep the lawn mower on the grass," and a warning, "or we will put it away." The final step would be to enforce a logical consequence if disobedience continued (willful or irresponsible). Later you could

discuss again, "We had to put the lawn mower away yesterday because you couldn't keep it on the grass," or "I was so proud that you remembered to keep your lawn mower on the grass after we talked about it." Commands and warnings only work if action follows immediately. Counting 1-2-3 is just a math lesson unless the child knows another tool will be used if he hasn't moved by number 3!

6. Ignore Selected Behaviors
Read James 1:19-20 and Colossians 3:12-13 in your Bible.
Some behaviors—sibling squabbles, whining, and tantrums—are aimed at getting attention. Others are tested just to see if there will be a favorable result. If the inappropriate behavior is minor, ignore it at first. Disrespectful, crude language or actions should not be ignored. Use a tool that communicates such behaviors will not happen again! "Remove the audience from the clown," was the most helpful advice we ever received. Within one month of taking this advice, our "clown" decided it wasn't much fun performing for an empty room!

7. Call Time-Out (Isolation)
Read Psalm 32:9 and Isaiah 30:15 in your Bible.
To "remove the *clown* from the *audience*" gives a child time to settle down, consider what has been done, or be restrained from inappropriate play (e.g. biting). A playpen, corner, or "thinking spot" can be used at home or away. Laying their head on a desk or having a silent ride in the car are other forms of time-out. If behavior is extremely disruptive, complete removal from the scene may be necessary. The amount of time needed varies by age, disposition, and the severity of the offense.

Ask, "What am I training?" when using this tool. For some children, being sent to their room is a reward! If siblings are getting extra attention, and the offender seems to be missing out on great fun, he will be motivated to redirect his actions and attitude to join the group again. Once the time-out is over, he should be welcomed back with positive words that encourage a good pattern. What about the child who won't stay in time-out, or never changes her behavior? Initially, you may need to train time-out using other tools (physical assistance, ignoring, or spanking). Once it is trained correctly, "Do you need time-out?" may be enough to cause a child headed for trouble to reconsider.

❦**Inside Look**
Verbalizing appropriate behavior has come in handy many times over the years. When the boys were spitting at each other, it worked great: "You can spit when you brush your teeth." When somebody else said "poo-poo head" at the table, I nonchalantly said, "When you want to use bathroom words, go to the bathroom." It kind of took the fun out of it, when I acknowledged that there might be an appropriate place for those words. I wasn't always so creative. At a picnic for a parenting class, we were talking about this tool, when my kids started fighting. I said, "Quit acting like brats." My young friend corrected me by verbalizing appropriate behavior: "Now use kind words!"—*Elaine*

69

One who looks intently at the perfect law, the law of liberty, and abides by it, not having become a forgetful hearer but an effectual doer, this man shall be blessed in what he does (James 1:25).

If we put the bits into the horses' mouths so that they may obey us, we direct their entire body as well. Behold, the ships also, though they are so great and are driven by strong winds, are still directed by a very small rudder, wherever the inclination of the pilot desires (James 3:3-4).

Since you know that you will receive an inheritance from the Lord as a reward. It is the Lord Christ you are serving. Anyone who does wrong will be repaid for his wrong, and there is no favoritism (Colossians 3:24-25).

8. Provide Physical Assistance
Read James 1:25 and 3:3-4.

Some children need a little boost to obey immediately and willingly. If you tell your child to put away his toys and he doesn't move, you might ask if he can do it himself or if he needs help. If he does not move, calmly place your hand over his and squeeze just enough, as you both pick up the toy, to make your kind of help uncomfortable. He will probably prefer to do it himself the next time. This is an effective approach for preschoolers who will not get up, pick up, hand over, stay seated, or come when called. Even our teenagers get moving when I offer such help on the count of three!

9. Remove Special Privileges
Read Colossians 3:24-25.

The older children get, the more they look forward to a variety of activities each day. These may include reading with parents, watching a television program, riding bikes, etc. Removal of a special privilege is a potent form of correction when it has been thought through ahead of time. "The television stays off since you didn't finish your homework." Following through on these is difficult, but so instructive! Be sure you are ready and able to enforce what you remove, especially if the privilege you take away penalizes the whole family.

⚙ **Review the tools for dealing with disobedience. Circle the ones you use with your children, given their ages and personalities. Underline those new to you and that you will try with your children.**

EVALUATE YOUR DISCIPLINE

Four questions will help you judge how successful your training has been and should be answered each time your child responds in obedience or disobedience. Be sure to read the Scripture in your Bible.

1. What did I train? *(Proverbs 1:2-6)*
When disciplining children, observe what was accomplished through instruction and correction.

2. Did I offend my child? *(Ephesians 6:4; Proverbs 15:1)*
Choose words carefully, and humbly show justice and mercy to your children.

3. Was my child repentant? *(2 Corinthians 7:10)*
True repentance is a change of heart characterized by honesty and confession; not a challenge of wits.

4. Is my child's spirit open? *(Colossians 3:21; Proverbs 17:22)*
A closed spirit manifests itself in the body (pulling away, resisting affection), in the soul (pouting, withdrawing, rejecting), and in the spirit (broken relationship, cutting family ties). Carefully and immediately restore an open spirit by: reflecting tenderness, increasing understanding, admitting offenses, attempting affection, and requesting forgiveness.

☼ **To help plant these questions in your mind, complete the four questions in the margin.**

Close your study by reflecting on the following quotation.

I LOVED YOU ENOUGH

Some day when my children are old enough to understand the logic that motivates a parent, I will tell them: I loved you enough to ask where you were going, with whom, and what time you would be home. I loved you enough to be silent and let you discover your new best friend was a creep. I loved you enough to make you take a Milky Way back to the drug store (with a bite out of it) and tell the clerk "I stole this yesterday and want to pay for it." I loved you enough to let you see anger, disappointment, and tears in my eyes. Children must learn that parents are not perfect. I loved you enough to let you assume the responsibility for your actions even when the penalties were so harsh they almost broke my heart. But most of all, I loved you enough to say NO when I knew you would hate me for it. Those were the most difficult battles of all. I am glad I won them, because in the end, you won something, too.[1]

EVALUATING DISCIPLINE

1. What did I _____?

2. Did I _____
  my child?

3. Was my child
  _____?

4. Is my child's _____
  open?

Parent Project 6

1. Observe each of your children this week and use these questions to evaluate the effectiveness of your discipline.
   - How responsible is he (consider action and attitude)?
   - How respectful is he (consider action and attitude)?
   - How teachable, honest, and repentant is he?
   - How is he unteachable, deceptive, or rebellious?
   - When he obeys, how does he respond to praise, affirmation, and rewards? What kind of rewards?

2. Try out a few of these each day this week and add some of your favorites.

Praising Performance

Good going!

Super!

I knew you could do it.

You are very good at that.

That's a fine job.

You've been practicing!

You did well today.

Keep it up!

You're really working hard today.

You remembered!

I like the way you …

You are doing beautifully.

Way to hang in there!

I like it when you . . .

Affirming Personhood

You're a winner.

I'm glad God gave you to me.

You are loving.

I love you no matter what.

You are a wonderful person.

You're awesome

There's no one like you!

You're the greatest.

You are kind.

You are special.

I'll always be here for you.

You're the best!

You make me happy!

You mean the world to me.

3. Write a letter to God about all you have learned about discipline. Be honest with God and tell Him where you need assistance. Ask His Spirit to illuminate your mind, refresh your creativity, and restore your strength to train up your children in His ways.

---

[1]"For Our Teenagers," *Pulpit Helps*, January 1992, 20.

Chapter 7
Handing Down Your Faith

PARENT VIEW 7

You are painting a picture of God for your children. What does your canvas look like?

⚏ Key Principle 1

Parents are called into _____ with God for spiritual

_____.

⚏ Key Principle 2

Teach _____ and principles about

_____ and His _____.

Truths and Principles About God and His Word

1. Share _____ and _____.

   • God's whole big name
   • God's creation, work, home, son, sacrifice

2. Teach your children to _____ God's Word.

   • _____ it.

   • _____ it.

   • _____ it.

   • _____ it.

SCRIPTURE USED DURING THE VIDEO SESSION ...
2 Timothy 1:5
Jeremiah 9:23-24
2 Timothy 3:14-15
3 John 4
Lamentations 2:19
Job 1:5

3. Present the _____ _____.

4. Let the _____ _____ do His work.

> Knowledge leads to Learning
> Learning leads to Conviction
> Conviction leads to Salvation

5. The _____ process never ends.

⌂ Key Principle 3

Prayer is the key to _____ our _____

to the next generation.

Kinds of Prayer

1. We must develop the discipline of praying _____

our children.

2. We also need to pray _____ our children.

Parent Talk 7

Use the following as a guide to talk with your spouse, another parent, or group of parents. Pray together as you begin your discussion.

1. Looking back over your childhood, what was your earliest "picture" of God? How has it changed during your life?

2. What stands out most about your spiritual training before age 12?

3. Who was the most spiritually influential person in your childhood? Why?

4. If God could be portrayed on canvas as you have painted Him for your children, what would He look like in their eyes?

5. What role did prayer play during your childhood? What role has it played since you became a parent?

6. If you are with a group of parents, break into small groups and give each group one question from the list below. In 10 minutes, come up with Scripture and a concrete object lesson, story, or illustration for each question. When time is up, ask each group to share the question and their group's response for each question. If you are doing Parent Talk 7 with your spouse or a friend, choose one or two of the questions to work on.

   • An eight year old who has not received Christ asks, "Why can't I take the Lord's supper?" or "When can I be baptized?"

   • A six year old who has not received Christ asks, "Am I a Christian?" or "When can I become a Christian?"

   • A four year old asks, "Why can't we see God?" or "Why can't Jesus come to my house?"

   • A five-year-old asks, "Who ends up in hell?" or "If I die, will I go to hell?"

Parent Shaper 7

❦Inside Look

A friend was in Russia to share Christ. As she boarded the bus to leave on her last day there, she looked out over the mob of people, their faces set as they marched through life. She felt compelled to call out a final message. In her loudest "mother's voice" and the little Russian she knew, she declared, "In the name of Jesus, I love you!" The response was shocking. The rush halted. People began looking around. Some were chanting. Others were crying. All were looking for the source of the news. A young man who spoke English shared the response of the people: "Say it again. Say it again. We haven't heard that name in so many years. Say it again!" How long will our window of opportunity stay open before there will be no one left to tell the good news to the next generation?—*Elaine*

Why is it important for our children to have faith in Christ? Do we understand and model faith in Christ for our children? This is what we will talk about in this chapter.

A Parent's Calling

Read Psalm 78:1-7 and 2 Corinthians 12:14-15 in your Bible.
Parents have been given the high calling to prepare their children to give their lives to Christ and to provide an atmosphere that promotes a hunger to know God. Too many parents believe the church should take the lead in spiritual instruction. Certainly, active commitment to a local congregation is beneficial, but it is a sobering thought that we are always just one generation away from "godlessness." Psalm 78 offers the key which opens the door of faith for the next generation.

⚙**What is your family's spiritual history? Trace your family's Christian heritage. Record this information on a separate sheet of paper to share with your children as they get older.**

Understand and Express Your Faith

Read Philippians 2:12 and 1 Peter 3:15 in your Bible.
To invite others to faith in Christ, we must understand it ourselves. Some Christians only generally recall how they came to know Christ. Entering into a covenant with God is compared with both marriage and adoption. We can go into detail about our wedding or the birth of our child. How can we hope to answer our children when our own salvation has not been "worked out"? We are commanded to be "ready to make a defense to everyone who asks you to give an account for the hope that is in you" (1 Peter 3:15).

☼**Write a statement that explains your faith in Christ.**

_____

_____

Model Your Faith
Read Ephesians 5:1-2 in your Bible.
Once I heard Paul Harvey say, "If you don't live it, you don't believe it." A Harvard University study found that amidst the high-tech sophistication of our world, the number one way to change lives is modeling. The best way to impact another life is to demonstrate, to practice, what one teaches.[1] Verbalizing our faith is important, but words mean nothing if we don't model our faith. We are to walk in love just as Christ did. If we don't live it, our children won't believe it!

☼**Reflect on this question: If the only gospel my child ever witnesses is my life, will he come to know Jesus?**

Children Are Born with an Openness to God
Read Matthew 18:6; 21:15; 2 Timothy 3:15; and 1 Samuel 1:24,28 in your Bible.
Young children can worship and glorify God, receive training, understand Scripture, believe, and come to Christ. The seeds sown during the preschool years can produce incredibly mature fruit during the school-age years. One reason adults may doubt that little children can digest spiritual truth is that so few have had the opportunity to taste much!

☼**What spiritual seeds have been sown in your children's lives?**

_____

_____

Children Are Born with a "Heart Defect"
Read Psalm 51:5; 58:3; and Romans 5:12 in your Bible.
Children do not become sinners because they sin. They sin because they are sinners, just like parents! As descendants of

TRUTHS OF THE GOSPEL MESSAGE

Grace—Romans 6:23, Ephesians 2:8. Heaven is a free gift from God. It is not earned or deserved.
Man—Romans 3:10-12,23; Titus 3:5; Proverbs 14:12. All are sinners and separated from God by sin. We cannot save ourselves.
God—Jeremiah 31:3; 1 John 4:8; Psalm 89:32; Exodus 34:7. God is merciful. God is just and must punish sin.
Jesus Christ—John 1:1; Isaiah 9:6; John 20:28; Isaiah 53:4,6; Romans 6:23. Jesus is the infinite God. Jesus paid for our sins and purchased a place in heaven for us.
Faith and Repentance—James 2:19; Matthew 8:29; Acts 16:31; John 3:36. Faith is not mere knowledge or intellectual agreement. Faith is trusting Christ alone for our salvation. Faith itself is a gift of God. Repentance is turning away from our sin and turning toward God. When we turn to God in repentance by faith, we find Him running toward us with outstretched arms.

Behold, all souls are Mine; the soul of the father as well as the soul of the son is Mine. The soul who sins will die. The son will not bear the punishment for the father's iniquity, nor will the father bear the punishment for the son's iniquity (Ezekiel 18:4,20).

When I was a child, I used to speak as a child, think as a child, reason as a child; when I became a man, I did away with childish things (1 Corinthians 13:11).

Adam, a spirit which is "dead to God" has been inherited. No one has to be taught to sin! Sin is "bound in the heart of a child," and it is revealed as soon as they learn to walk and talk. No medicine or therapy can change the outcome. The only hope is a heart "transplant."

Children Will Become Accountable for Sin (but When?)

Read Ezekiel 18:4,20 and 1 Corinthians 13:11.

We naturally want to help our children make the right choices. But the day will come when every person must present his life to God. Scripture does not specify an "age of accountability," but implies there is a period of time before children can know to refuse evil and choose good. How long they are safe, only God knows. We must continue diligently preparing their minds to receive the entire gospel when they are able to grasp it.

☼ **What would you do differently if you knew the "age of accountability"?**

_____

_____

Our Role with Young Children

Read 1 Samuel 2:18,21,26; 3:4,7-8,10-11 in your Bible.

In our urgency for their souls to be saved, we must never push a child to profess a faith that has not taken root. They must know they are being called to respond to God alone. Most 5 year olds would "ask Jesus into their heart" if pressed: "God loves you so much, and Jesus wants to live with you forever. Don't you want to invite Him into your heart?" If they have heard the song "Jesus Loves Me" since the womb, of course they will. Samuel's story is an inspiration for parents of younger children. Samuel was ministering before the Lord as a little boy and was attentive and obedient enough to be aware of someone calling him. However, he "did not yet know the Lord, nor had the word of the Lord yet been revealed to him" (1 Samuel 3:7). It took a wiser adult (Eli) to discern that it was God calling to the boy. Eli's role was to instruct Samuel how to respond when God called him again.

A Concept You Can't Teach

Read Psalm 34:11-15 in your Bible.

We can teach children how to revere God. We can teach them to identify sin and its traps. We can teach them to pursue the ways of love and peace, but we cannot force the timing or manufacture conviction and sorrow over personal sin. If they aren't sure how to define sin, how can they be saved from it? This is both good news and bad news. If they cannot identify sin at whatever age they are, they are probably still safe. When they can give you a list that sounds quite personalized, they are getting closer! This is when God's role intensifies. We continue to plant and water, while His Holy Spirit is deep within, developing the root system.

☀ **What is your child's awareness of sin—by definition or by his own experience? Explain.**

_____

_____

Share Truths and Principles About God

Read Genesis 4:7; Acts 4:12; and Philippians 3:8 in your Bible.

God longs to take possession of children before sin masters them. A perfect beginning point is to learn what God has told us about Himself in the Bible: His name(s), His creation, His work, His home, His Son, and His sacrifice. This progression lends itself to questions and discussions about sin, forgiveness, and salvation. When Amanda was young, she loved to hear the meaning of each of her names. This confirmed that she belonged and had a special identity. She always asked people their names, but if they gave only their first name she would ask, "No, what's your whole big name?" We forgot about her game until we began studying the 200 plus names of God in Scripture. That study provided a springboard for teaching our children to get to know God. His work in the world and in history confirms His sovereignty. His home opens a big can of worms—especially when you get to the part about what will (and won't) be in heaven. "Will Fluffy be in heaven?" "Will toys be in heaven?" "What about people who don't love Jesus?" After my grandmother died, we were flying home, and when we went

❤Inside Look

When the boys were six years old, we were praying for the ability to answer clearly the questions that were coming almost daily. The extremes of behavior had become noticeable, with more conflict and emotion, yet more tenderness and sensitivity. One week before he received Christ, Joel was having trouble sleeping. He asked Blake, "Do you ever hear God calling you?" Blake responded, "I don't know." Joel said, "I think God has been calling me." Elaine interrupted, "What is God saying?" He said, "I think to become a Christian." Elaine asked why he thought God would call him to do that. Joel answered, "Because I've sinned and I'm not one." We talked, shared Scripture, asked questions, and prayed; he prayed and offered Jesus his life. His first two thoughts were of who he needed to tell and of his desire to pray for his brother, Blake.
—David and Elaine

through the clouds Amanda asked, "Is this where Honey got out?" The rest, as they say, is history! By school age, kids may know every story about Jesus, but they will become more curious about the details of the cross and its meaning.

☼ **Which of God's names can you use to introduce your child to Him? Start a list in the margin (*for example: Bread of Life, Deliverer, Helper*).**

Teach Children to Value God's Word
Read 2 Timothy 3:14-15 and Psalm 119:18 in your Bible.
Paul reminded Timothy how Scripture led him to salvation and wisdom. "From childhood" actually means from infancy. Every time you open a Bible, remind your children that this book contains true stories God told people to write. Don't worry that children can't interpret every verse. When they hear verses they have sung or memorized in conversations or sermons, their ears will perk up! Your job is to plant the seeds. God will bring His words to their remembrance later (see John 14:26). As they listen, they will "become convinced" because children don't need a course in apologetics to accept spiritual truth. Children who see their parents excited about studying and obeying God's Word will receive it with the same enthusiasm.

A Lifetime of Discipleship
Read 2 Kings 22; 23:1-3,25 and 2 Chronicles 34 in your Bible.
Notice how close the word *disciple* is to *discipline*. Once children become Christians, you must continue the cycle of training that began during the early years. The goal is salvation and Christlikeness. Josiah's story is great encouragement for Christian parents who did not have this kind of spiritual training at home—or who worry that teenagers can't increase in their faith. Josiah's father and grandfather "did evil in the sight of the Lord" (2 Kings 21:20). When Amon was murdered, his son, Josiah, became king. He was only 8 years old, so who trained him to do "right in the sight of the Lord" (2 Kings 22:2)? One key may be the inclusion of the names of his mother and maternal grandfather. Josiah began to seek the God of his forefathers when he was 16. By age 20, he was bold enough to purge Judah of pagan worship. When he was 26, the discovery of the "whole purpose of God" (Acts 20:27) changed his life and the lives of a

NAMES OF GOD

_____

_____

_____

_____

_____

_____

❦Inside Look
Last Christmas, Elaine was looking for something "spiritual" to do on Christmas Eve. She thought the kids might spend half an hour making a garland for the tree with some names of God on it. Several hours later, amid tape, glitter, markers, and glue, they had recalled over 100 of the names of God and wrapped the entire downstairs with a border which declared God's "whole big name"!
—*David*

nation. First Kings 13:1-2 contains the prophesy of Josiah's birth and God's strategic placement of him in that generation. God can completely change a family tree in one generation!

☼**Reflect on this question: Could it be that God has strategically placed your child in this generation?**

The Greatest Gift of Parenting: Prayer
Read Colossians 4:2 and Lamentations 2:19.
A senator was asked to address the annual men's dinner at a local church. About 450 men were present. During the meal, the issue of school prayer came up. The senator asked two questions. "How many of you would like to see prayer restored to the public schools?" As far as he could tell, every hand was raised with many "Amens!" "How many of you pray with your children every morning at home?" The silence was embarrassing. He pointed out how interesting it is that we talk about the importance of prayer, yet actually do it so little.[2]

☼**What has been your practice of praying for your children? Explain.**

_____

_____

Praying for and with Our Children
Read James 5:16 and 1 Samuel 1:27-28; 2:1-11 in your Bible.
It is pleasing to God when you lift your children to His throne, but picture His delight when you accompany them there. Praying for your children is powerful and effective. Praying with your children teaches them how to walk with God and trains them how to talk with Him. They need to overhear conversations with the Heavenly Father, then to join in themselves.

☼**Have your children ever observed you praying? Have your children ever asked you to pray with them about a concern? Make a commitment to God to be more visible with your prayer life.**

Devote yourselves to prayer, keeping alert in it with an attitude of thanksgiving (Colossians 4:2).

*"Arise, cry aloud in the night
At the beginning of the night watches;
Pour out your heart like water
Before the presence of the Lord;
Lift up your hands to Him
For the life of your little ones"
(Lamentations 2:19).*

It is much easier to train a child to pray, because they are more humble and uninhibited than adults. Stuart Hampel and Eric Marshall compiled a book called *Children 's Letters to God: The New Collection* with some of the following excerpts:

Dear God: Are you really invisible or is that just a trick? *Lucy*
Dear God: It is great the way you always get the stars in the right places. *Jeff*
Dear God: I'm doing the best I can. *Frank*
Dear God: Thank you for the baby brother but what I prayed for was a puppy. *Joyce*[3]

MY PRAYER FOR MY CHILD

_____

_____

_____

"Believe in the Lord Jesus, and you shall be saved, you and your household" (Acts 16:31).

What Should I Pray?

Read Job 1:1-5 and 1 Chronicles 29:17-19 in your Bible.
Even now that our children have received Christ as their Savior, our praying continues. Parents never quit praying for their children. Who else will show such concern until this generation takes up its charge for the next one? Even when his children were grown, Job would rise up early in the morning and present offerings to the Lord on their behalf. What did he pray? Job was concerned that " 'perhaps my sons have sinned and cursed God in their hearts' " (Job 1:5). Job wasn't praying about their health, prosperity, or circumstances. He was focused on the condition of their hearts. David prayed for Solomon in a like manner and asked that he would have a "perfect heart" (1 Chronicles 29:19) to keep the Lord's commandments. David knew that wisdom begins in the inner person, before it is revealed in outward behavior.

What have you been praying for your children? List three things in the margin you would like God to do in their lives.

Praying God's Will Through His Word

Read Acts 16:31 and 31 Daily Petitions (pp. 84-85).
No surer words can be found than praying for your children directly from Scripture. When you pray God's words, you can have absolute confidence that you are in agreement with Him. In *The Man in the Mirror,* Patrick Morley tells of 7 couples, all new Christians, who started meeting in a prayer group. The results of their prayers were so dramatic that he verified their story with three separate sources. It seems these "naive" new Christians discovered a verse of Scripture and decided to claim it as a promise from God. The verse was Acts 16:31. Among the 7 couples, they had 23 children, none of whom were Christians at the time. Each week the couples would faithfully pray for the salvation of their beloved children. Over the course of 2 years, all 23 committed their lives to Jesus Christ.[4]

Oswald Chambers said, "One of the blessed things about this life is that a man carries his [God's] kingdom on the inside, and that makes the outside lovely."[5] As we close this study, may we continually pray for God to build a great kingdom within our children so lovely it would truly shape the next generation!

Parent Project 7

There are more exercises here than you can do in one week, so choose some you wish to incorporate over the next several weeks and months.

1. Take the "spiritual temperature" in your home by measuring the subjects of your daily conversations. Be aware of how much family conversation centers around spiritual things. Don't count family devotionals.

2. Start every day by asking, "I wonder what God is going to do today?" and allow your children's imaginations to run wild!

3. Choose a character quality from your blueprint. Have older children do a Scripture search for verses about that quality. Encourage them to discover an example of the quality (or the lack of it) at school, in the neighborhood, on television, etc. At the end of your week or during a family time, have each child share what they've learned.

4. Children can learn 26 verses in 6 months by memorizing a verse per week corresponding with each letter of the alphabet.

5. Have a car rider in a certain seat open a Bible to the verse you marked the night before. Invite children to interpret its meaning and apply it for the day. Incorporate the verse into a prayer for the day.

6. Go around the table at meal time and let each person say "Thank you God for …" Teach the concept of praise using the names of God. "I love you God because you are …" (holy, my rock, faithful and true). Model confession with, "God, I want to tell on myself that … (allow the confession to be silent or aloud). Emphasize that God will always love us but is sad over the wrong things we do. Help children begin looking outward by praying for others (intercession).

[1]Tim Hansel, *Sermons Illustrated* (Holland, OH: Jeff and Pam Carroll, September 1990).

[2]David and Elaine Atchison, *Shaping the Next Generation Leader's Guide* (Fort Worth: Turning Point, 1992), 118-19.

[3]Stuart Hample and Eric Marshall, compilers, *Children's Letters to God: The New Collection* (New York: Workman Publishing, 1991), 8, 37, 83, 89.

[4]David McCasland, *Oswald Chambers: Abandoned to God* (Oswald Chambers Publication Association, 1993), 118.

31 DAILY PETITIONS

1. Angels' protection. *"For He will command His angels concerning you to guard you in all your ways"* (Psalm 91:11).

2. A genuine conversion. *"From infancy you have known the holy Scriptures, which are able to make you wise for salvation through faith in Christ Jesus"* (2 Timothy 3:15).

3. A sense of destiny. *" 'For I know the plans I have for you,' declares the Lord, 'plans to prosper you and not to harm you, plans to give you hope and a future' "* (Jeremiah 29:11).

4. Grow in faith. *"Yet he [Abraham] did not waver through unbelief regarding the promise of God, but was strengthened in his faith and gave glory to God, being fully persuaded that God had power to do what He had promised"* (Romans 4:20-21).

5. Submission to God. *"Therefore, I urge you, brothers, in view of God's mercy, to offer your bodies as living sacrifices, holy and pleasing to God—this is your spiritual act of worship"* (Romans 12:1).

6. Power over sin. *"We died to sin; how can we live in it any longer? … For sin shall not be your master, because you are not under law, but under grace"* (Romans 6:2,14).

7. Please God in every way. *"We pray this … that you may live a life worthy of the Lord and may please Him in every way: bearing fruit in every good work"* (Colossians 1:10).

8. Respect for authority. *"He who rebels against the authority is rebelling against what God has instituted"* (Romans 13:2).

9. Teachable spirit. *"Let the wise listen and add to their learning, and let the discerning get guidance … Listen, my son, to your father's instruction and do not forsake your mother's teaching"* (Proverbs 1:5,8).

10. Increasing spiritual maturity. *"Let us leave the elementary teachings about Christ and go on to maturity"* (Hebrews 6:1).

11. Wisdom. *"Choose my instruction instead of silver, knowledge rather than choice gold, for wisdom is more precious than rubies, and nothing you desire can compare with her"* (Proverbs 8:10-11).

12. Discerning truth from error. *"So give your servant a discerning heart … to distinguish between right and wrong"* (1 Kings 3:9).

13. Integrity. *"We have conducted ourselves in the world, and especially in our relations with you, in the holiness and sincerity that are from God"* (2 Corinthians 1:12).

14. Moral Purity. *"Flee from sexual immorality … Do you not know that your body is a temple of the Holy Spirit … ?"* (1 Corinthians 6:18-19).

15. Courage. *"Be strong and courageous. Do not be terrified; do not be discouraged, for the Lord your God will be with you wherever you go"* (Joshua 1:9).

16. Perseverance. *"Stand firm. Let nothing move you. Always give yourselves fully to the work of the Lord … your labor in the Lord is not in vain"* (1 Corinthians 15:58).

17. Self-discipline. *"Train yourself to be godly. For physical training is of some value, but godliness has value for all things, holding promise for both the present life and the life to come"* (1 Timothy 4:7-8).

18. Usefulness to God. *"Make every effort to add to your faith goodness; and to goodness, knowledge; and to knowledge, self-control; and to self-control, perseverance; and to perseverance, godliness; and to godliness, brotherly kindness; and to brotherly kindness, love. For it you possess these qualities in increasing measure, they will keep you from being ineffective and unproductive in your knowledge of our Lord Jesus Christ"* (2 Peter 1:5-8).

19. A sensitive heart. *"As God's chosen people, holy and dearly loved, clothe yourselves with compassion, kindness, humility, gentleness and patience"* (Colossians 3:12).

20. A cheerful heart. *"A cheerful heart is good medicine"* (Proverbs 17:22).

21. A serving heart. *"Your attitude should be the same as that of Christ Jesus: Who … made Himself nothing, taking the very nature of a servant"* (Philippians 2:5-7).

22. A grateful heart. *"Rejoice in the Lord, you who are righteous, and praise his holy name"* (Psalm 97:12).

23. Perspective on possessions. *"Godliness with contentment is great gain. For we brought nothing into the world, and we can take nothing out of it. But if we have food and clothing, we will be content with that"* (1 Timothy 6:6-8).

24. Pursuit of excellence. *"Whatever you do, work at it with all your heart, as working for the Lord, not for men"* (Colossians 3:23).

25. Protection from the evil one. *"'My prayer is not that You take them out of the world but that You protect them from the evil one'"* (John 17:15).

26. Overcome Satan's temptation. *"Because He Himself suffered when he was tempted, He is able to help those who are being tempted"* (Hebrews 2:18).

27. Avoid negative influences. *"My son, if sinners entice you, do not give in to them. … my son, do not go along with them, do not set foot on their paths"* (Proverbs 1:10,15).

28. Godly friends. *"Then Daniel returned to his house and explained the matter to his friends … He urged them to plead for mercy from the God of heaven … Then Nebuchadnezzar said, 'Praise be to the God of Shadrach, Meshach and Abednego, who … trusted in Him … and were willing to give up their lives rather than serve or worship any god except their own God"* (Daniel 2:17-18, 3:28).

29. Godly life partner. *"Do not be yoked together with unbelievers. For what do right-eousness and wickedness have in common? Or what fellowship can light have with darkness?"* (2 Corinthians 6:14).

30. A consistent walk. *"Blessed is the man who does not walk in the counsel of the wicked or stand in the way of sinners or sit in the seat of mockers. But his delight is in the law of the Lord, and on his law he meditates day and night. He is like a tree planted by streams of water, which yields its fruit in season and whose leaf does not wither"* (Psalm 1:1-3).

31. Long, prosperous life. *"My son, do not forget my teaching, but keep my commands in your heart, for they will prolong your life many years and bring you prosperity"* (Proverbs 3:1-2).

OPEN LETTERS TO HURTING PARENTS

Our lives don't always fit into neat packages, and there are always issues that can't be covered in a study with such a broad scope. So we have included five open letters addressing issues that come up most often when we are with parents.

For Parents of Children with ADD or ADHD

Though Attention Deficit Disorder (ADD) is often misdiagnosed, it does exist! There is a great deal of misunderstanding about the diagnosis and treatment of this neurodevelopmental disorder, which affects three to five percent of the population and often runs in families. Inattention, impulsivity, and hyperactivity are just a few of the symptoms which vary between children, often leaving parents and caregivers exhausted and exasperated. Unfortunately, these behaviors may resemble other emotional and behavioral problems or learning disabilities. Many parents feel frustration and guilt when friends or teachers insist that better discipline is the answer. Even when disciplined correctly, these children require more structure, extreme consistency, and unique strategies. Children with ADD or ADHD (with hyperactivity) often suffer a significant loss of self-esteem by the time they are diagnosed and treated. Many have already been labeled as troublemakers by adults who have unintentionally reinforced their negative responses.

Stimulant medications are often used to improve concentration and decrease impulsive or aggressive behaviors, but child management is also a critical component. Children with ADHD need more individual attention, affirmation, opportunities for active participation, and consistent routines. They need to obtain information in creative ways, and often respond well to multimedia instruction. Positive consequences should be the first approach. Loving messages must be communicated regardless of behavior. Tangible rewards, charts, and contracts are good reinforcers that lead to small steps of progress.

Tools like verbal feedback, single warnings, restatement of rules, and natural or logical consequences should be used after inappropriate behavior. For hitting or aggression, do not warn, but use a five-minute time-out with no form of attention, silently adding minutes to a timer for each disruption. Three key words are *immediate, mild,* and *consistent.* Severe punishment and angry responses tend to backfire with these children. They are especially sensitive to being singled out and embarrassed in front of their peers.

Schools are required to adapt to each child's needs, but some schools (even churches) are inflexible when difficult children disrupt their programming. Christian friends should listen to parent concerns, then commit to learn more, support more, and adapt more. Churches can begin by gathering resources and offering support groups and seminars. These provide both inreach and outreach opportunities. These parents need patience, encouragement, and the ministry of baby-sitting at least once a month! All children need to be equally welcomed and nurtured within a safe and accepting community that goes beyond what schools are required to offer. God loves us because we belong to Him, not based on our performance or behavior. We are called by God to do no less.

For Further Support

- Galvin, Matthew R. *Otto Learns About His Medicine: A Story about Medication for Children with ADHD*. Washington, DC: American Psychological Association, 1995.
- Gordon, Michael. *Jumpin' Johnny Get Back to Work! A Child's Guide to ADHD— Hyperactivity*. DeWitt, NY: GSI Publications, 1991.
- Kajander, Rebecca. *Living with ADHD: A Practical Guide to Coping with Attention Deficit Hyperactivity Disorder*. Minneapolis: Park Nicollet Medical Foundation, 1995.
- Kennedy, Patricia, et al. *The Hyperactive Child Book: Treating, Educating, and Living with an ADHD Child*. New York: St. Martin's Press, 1993.
- *Children and Adults with Attention Deficit Disorders* (CH.A.D.D.); 499 NW 70th Avenue, Suite 101; Plantation, FL 33317; (800) 233-4050; www.chadd.org

For Single Moms and Dads

More than half of American children will spend time in a single-parent home before reaching adulthood. Because of divorce, there are over 12 million female-headed, single-parent homes and 1.2 million male-headed, single-parent homes in the United States. Today there are almost as many never-married single mothers as divorced mothers. Widowed moms and dads comprise only about 5 percent of the single parent population but face some unique challenges within single parenting.

Both divorce and death cause shock and grief, but losing a spouse through death shakes a person's world in unique ways. There is no "ex," no betrayal, and often, no warning. Immediate responsibilities may postpone the normal grieving process. Denial, anger, guilt, or false acceptance may come before true acceptance. A child's grief tends to be more open-ended, especially when they are not old enough to process such abstract concepts. Adults and children need to allow themselves adequate time to grieve. Keeping the same structure and routine may help make things seem more "normal." Allow children to talk, ask questions, and express emotions. Attend a grief support group through a church or in the community. Ultimately, only God can help us make sense of our pain—and He has promised to comfort and father the fatherless (see Matthew 5:4, Psalm 68:5-6).

Divorce leaves adults and children with a different sense of loss. Usually, divorced parents' lives continue to intersect. About 90 percent of mothers receive custody of the children, but there are continuing legalities regarding custody, visitation, and child support. There are economic stressors and over half who are due child support don't get it. The change in roles and responsibilities lead to increased parenting stressors. Problems with money and role/task overload are the most common dilemmas reported by single mothers. The physical and emotional burdens, besides being single again, lead to social stressors. Problems with their former spouse and role/task overload are the top two obstacles noted by single fathers. All of these create the need for a supportive network of adults. Establishing these relationships seems to be more difficult for single dads, perhaps because most are the noncustodial parent. The needs of each person in the broken family circle must be considered, because each one is hurting in a different way.

When custody is shared, both parents must work to be gracious and respect the rules in the other home. For the children's sake, save important discussions with your former mate for private times. Accommodate the other parent whenever possible. The most common complaints of children are negative talk from both parents about the other, cancellations or no shows by the visiting parent, and disagreements between Mom and Dad about how to raise the kids. Collaborating is always best for the children, but you cannot control how your former spouse responds. You can only work on how you respond. Agree to a win-win situation for everyone. Acknowledge that conflict is common in every home. Noncustodial parents report more anxiety, depression, and stress-related illnesses than custodial parents. Those who wish to be a part of their children's lives need to hear this message: Don't withdraw. Your children need you more than ever. Live as close as possible. Invest everything you have in continued influence on your children. Stay in weekly touch with them and attend school and extracurricular activities. Invite them to call, email, or write any time. Support discipline in the custodial home. Pray for them every day, remembering that God takes better care of our children than we can.

The single parent's number one goal is to create a safe, secure environment for the children. It helps children know that in spite of the differences that led to separation, both parents will continue to help and guide them. Request support from extended family, and remember that the church family counts, too! Many offer support groups and ministry to both parents and children. Explore options such as job-sharing, part-time, flextime, or working at home. Together, we must help our children break the cycle of unhealthy patterns from the past. Joel 2:25 states that there is nothing God can't redeem or restore. Don't let any person or circumstance rob you of that hope.

For Further Support
- Burkett, Larry. *The Financial Guide for the Single Parent.* Chicago: Moody, 1997.
- Davis, Verdell. *Let Me Grieve, but Not Forever.* Dallas, TX: Word, 1997.
- Hunter, Lynda. *Parenting on Your Own.* Grand Rapids, MI: Zondervan, 1997.
- Cindy Ann Pitts. *KidShare: What Do I Do Now?* Nashville: LifeWay Press, 1994.

For Grandparents Helping Parent Their Grandchildren

God reserves special blessings for over 3 million American grandparents who are raising their grandchildren. The census predicts millions more play a primary role in parenting, and the number will grow to 13 to 14 million by the year 2000. Nineties grandparents play a different role than previous grandparents. Grandparents are getting younger every day! Most are healthier, busier, and working longer. Some play their roles beautifully. Others have chosen not to grandparent because of past experiences. A large number would admit that grandparenting in this decade is not as *grand* as they dreamed.

Divorce is the biggest problem facing Christian grandparents today. How can a grandparent support their grandchildren of divorce? Grandparents can provide positive male/female role models for children who have distracted or absent moms and dads. Some grandparents are even foster grandparents to children who are not their own. Irene Endicott, author and grandmother of 12, advises grandparents to let the parents focus on their problems. Meanwhile, grandparents can focus on the grandchildren by reassuring them, valuing them, and keeping an unbiased attitude toward both parents. Some grandparents can provide services for single, working parents, including day care, daily prayer, a weekly home-cooked meal, running errands, or picking up the children for an afternoon of fun. When the grandchildren are with grandparents, they should maintain a normal routine. Grandparents may be the only stabilizing factor in their lives. But grandparents must not forget to take care of their own health and marriage! They must draw appropriate boundaries, knowing they cannot solve every problem.

Many grandparents are parenting their grandchildren due to a parent's substance, physical, emotional, or sexual abuse; abandonment; death; illness; or imprisonment. Grandparents may need to offer physical and emotional refuge during difficult periods. Before allowing or inviting an adult child and/or grandchildren to stay in their home, grandparents must carefully pray about their role, plan how permanent the situation will be, and partner with the adult child to create and honor guidelines within their home.

The call to parent again requires adjustments and sacrifices. Parenting grandparents admit to emotions ranging from anger and grief to guilt or self-pity. There are often conflicts between Grandmother and Grandfather about child rearing the second time around. Grandparents may need financial advisors, parenting classes, church family and community support, and prayer. Many will need a competent attorney in family law to deal with custody, adoption, and mediation issues. Grandparent support groups can help reduce stress, develop a network between grandparents, and provide opportunities to share the unique issues and emotions they face.

Consider the call to bless your adult children and grandchildren. It's never too late for godly grandparents to reconnect the legacy of blessing for future generations. Pray for the next three generations—your grandchildren, your great grandchildren, and your great-great grandchildren. Today's grandparents can make the difference in their grandchildren's lives!

For Further Support
• Endicott, Irene M. *Grandparenting by Grace.* Book. Nashville, TN: Broadman & Holman, 1994.

- Endicott, Irene M. *Grandparenting by Grace.* Interactive study. Nashville, TN: LifeWay Press, 1994.
- AARP Grandparent Information Center; 601 E. Street NW; Washington, DC 20001; 1-202-434-2296.

For Parents of Children with Special Needs

I can't believe this is happening to me. How can I handle this? What will happen to my child and my family? What did I do to cause this? What about all my hopes and dreams? This isn't fair! Why did this happen? All of these are common questions and emotions experienced by parents who are raising a medically fragile or disabled child. These parents are grieving the death of the universal dream of "the perfect child." One writer compared these feelings to planning an exciting vacation to Italy, but on arrival hearing, "Welcome to Holland." You must find new guidebooks, learn a new language, and realize that there is beautiful scenery in this place as well—though it's not what you anticipated.

"Fearfully and wonderfully made" (Psalm 139:14) may cause questions as you face the daily realities of illness or impairment. Your immediate priority is the best possible medical care and intervention. A federal program has made evaluation, therapy, and infant stimulation available for every significantly-delayed infant aged birth to three. At age three, your public school system is required to provide an appropriate developmental preschool setting and therapy until the child reaches school age. Begin to educate yourself right away so you don't miss opportunities that will make a difference in years to come.

A second priority is to allow yourself time to grieve. Don't deny your feelings. Dads seem to have a harder time in the beginning, because they don't cry or talk about their feelings as readily as moms. Men want to take action and fix things, while women need to feel protected and comforted. It is common for ongoing demands, financial strain, lack of time together as a couple, and normal male-female differences to cause distance between you. You must learn to cling together when your life feels torn apart. Approximately 85 percent of the marriages of couples with a special-needs child end in divorce.

Ninety percent of the direct care for special needs children is carried out by mothers. Dads who get involved with this care find more responsive wives in the long run. It's hard—at first—to see beyond tubes or wheelchairs or blank stares into the beautiful inner person of every child. God knows what it is like to ache for a hurting child, and the Bible tells us He actually keeps our tears in a bottle and records them in His Book (Psalm 56:8). When you are too tired or burdened to pray, read the Psalms aloud to each other. Pray Scripture over your child. Write a letter to God and journal the concerns and questions that will help another parent in the future. God wants to use you to minister to other parents in ways no other person could. One of our greatest joys is to be a part of the healing process with young parents who are just beginning their journey.

A third priority is finding a support system as soon as possible. The needs of a child with severe medical or developmental problems can consume the lives of the entire family. Sometimes the most difficult obstacle is educating family members so they can and will provide support. Parents should involve and inform grandparents, but be considerate of their time and aware that they are grieving, too. Grandparents must move beyond fears and attitudes like "we've never had anything like this on our side of the family," to see that they can be one of the most strengthening ties in this child's life. To move beyond living only in the survival mode, both parents need regular interaction with other parents in the same situation. Special parent groups were our greatest source of information and encouragement during the early years. There are many opportunities within communities—and on the Internet—to exchange facts and give hope to parents around the world. There are also sibling support groups which allow brothers and sisters an outlet to discuss feelings toward the child with special needs and for parents who are overburdened.

In an ideal world, your church family will reach out in love for you, although most must be taught how to minister to "extraordinary kids." Don't be afraid to answer when someone asks, "What can I do?" Ideas include: cook a meal; take other children to a special event; come one morning to change sheets; do laundry; vacuum floors; or watch the special child in the home while Mom and Dad spend time doing other tasks.

Two questions to church leaders: Why aren't there more disabled people at church? Why don't parents bring their children with special needs? Churches must take the initiative to be accessible, to offer extended care during the worship service, and to include every child in all activities. Having some time away is vital to the sanity and overall health of the family. Include respite care at least once a month and train volunteers to stay with a medically fragile child at home so parents can attend worship. A distinction of Christian support groups is prayer. Consider the evangelistic opportunity of opening your doors to hurting parents in your community. Remember, most families will not ask for help but will accept it when offered. When we meet Jesus, will He be able to say, "For I had Down Syndrome and you taught me; I had cerebral palsy and you listened to me; I had AIDS and you comforted me … Truly I say to you, to the extent that you did it to one of these brothers of Mine, *even the least of them,* you did it to Me" (Matthew 35:35-46)?

For Further Support

- Fuller, Cheri and Louise Tucker Jones. *Extraordinary Kids*. Colorado Springs: Focus on the Family, 1997.
- Wright, Norm and Joyce Wright. *I'll Love You Forever.* Colorado Springs: Focus on the Family, 1993.
- National Information Center for Children and Youth with Disabilities; P.O. Box 1492; Washington, DC 20013-1492; (800) 695-0285; email: nichcy@aed.org; www.nichcy.org
- Parents Helping Parents: Parent-Directed Family Resource Center for Children with Special Needs; 3041 Olcott Street; Santa, Clara, CA 95054-3222; (408) 727-5775; email: info@php.com; www.php.com

For Parents in Blending Families

Perhaps the most complex parenting atmosphere is the blended—or "blending"—family. There is no easy formula for grafting two direct households, one or more indirect households, a web of extended families, and all the relationships that emerge. These families need the support of their church and other blended families who have "beat the odds" by God's unfailing grace. Knowing what to do is much easier than living it out!

Typical obstacles shared by each blended family member are loyalty conflicts between biological parents/children and stepparents/stepchildren; loss, anger, and insecurity from the past; loving nonbiological parents/children as much as their own; and conflict with the other household(s). We can only address a few of these needs here.

Virtually every family member acknowledges uneasy feelings and displaced identity. Stepparents will not instantly (in some cases, never) love nonbiological children as their own. Stepchildren past the age of four or five have already bonded to their biological parent, and often view the new parent as a threat to that bond. Children must be given time and space to process each new relationship. Sudden change should be avoided. One of the most difficult rearrangements is the birth orders of the biological children and the stepchildren. To address this issue, sit down together and draw your family "constellation." Are there now two "firstborn" children? Has your "baby" been dethroned by a younger stepsibling? Older children operate in modes developed through years of finding their place and identity within one family. There are sure to be "collisions" when you move their branch in the family tree.

Not every family problem is caused by blending! However, some tasks will be more challenging in blending families. The most important way to build a secure and stable family is for husband and wife to commit to loving each other and developing a strong Christian marriage. It is more difficult to focus on couple bonding when children come with the marriage. You must learn to effectively communicate and resolve conflict. There may be unexpected ambushes from the past which reveal "baggage" that was never unpacked. Child rearing disagreements are the greatest contributor to second-marriage breakups. Children need united, consistent discipline from a coparenting team. This is a critical area to work through. Learn to give equal status to biological and nonbiological parents by putting up a united front. Balance leniency and harshness, and provide consistency by both adults. This will tell your children that they can count on both of you for structure and nurture.

Learn about the team building technique of resolving conflict, where every person has a voice to express his position, explore his concerns, and select mutually acceptable solutions. That leads to the ultimate task of family bonding. Some families will never blend. But you can control your responses—forgiving everyone who has wronged you, accepting each person's unique identity, looking at life through the eyes of each person, investing yourself in everyone's activities, and "rewriting" family traditions. Blending a family takes time—to stop analyzing and overreacting to every action of another, to make and carry out rules for your home, to work with the other household for the sake of the children. Joel 2:25 promises that God wants to restore the years the "swarming locust" has eaten. Ask God to restore His design for blending families.

For Further Support

- Frydenger, Tom and Adrienne Frydenger. *Stepfamily Problems: How to Solve Them.* Ada, MI: Fleming H. Revell, 1997.
- Dunn, Dick. *New Faces in the Frame: A Guide to Marriage and Parenting in the Blended Family*. Nashville: LifeWay Press, 1997.
- Leman, Kevin. *Living in a Stepfamily Without Getting Stepped On.* Nashville: Thomas Nelson, 1994.

For Married Parents

Many professionals in parenting have said the greatest gift you can give your children is a good marriage. *Right from Wrong* reported that less than half of Christian youth wanted to model their marriage after their parents, and more than a third said they definitely do not want a relationship like their parents.[1] One of the most immediate and difficult challenges we face is balancing our roles as an individual, spouse, and parent. Especially during our children's early years, our identity as individuals and spouses is easily neglected. Moms feel pulled by someone constantly needing her, plus household (and often workplace) demands. By the end of the day, a husband may find his wife seemingly oblivious—or resentful—of his needs. Meanwhile she is wondering, *What about my needs?* Young dads are frequently at a critical point in their careers when children arrive. Downsizing has doubled everyone's workload and raised concern about job security. Dad may be thinking, *Doesn't anybody appreciate how hard I work?* Unfortunately, there's usually no time to answer those questions in a busy home!

Children won't wait, but neither will marriages. Your relationship may either move from intimacy to isolation, or from partnership to parallel lives before your kids get out of diapers. Don't rationalize that things will get better when the kids go to school, or during the teenage years, or when they all finally leave the nest. Respond while there is still time. One of the first steps is to take a closer look at each of your roles.

Individual—When was the last time you honestly said that you love your life? How vigilant have you been about your spiritual, emotional, and physical health (in that order)? Part of your role as an individual includes your vocation. Is it in proper priority after your relationships with God, spouse, and children?

Parent—A great deal of resentment and bitterness can spring up when one spouse believes they have earned the right to relax, or be released from responsibility because they have "had a hard day." The other spouse will be much more cordial and responsive if they pitch in with dinnertime, bath time, and bedtime. In many homes, working moms still do most of the daily household and parenting tasks along with their outside jobs. No wonder our relationships are weakened! Attention, full-time, stay-at-home parents! You aren't "just a mom" (or dad)! Agree with your spouse on both of your "working hours." After that time, coparent and complete tasks as a team.

Spouse—How have you nurtured your relationship with your mate over the course of your marriage? During the last year? This week? Would you describe your marriage as growing, stagnant, or vibrant? How do you think your spouse would answer?

Think about what first attracted you to your mate. Consider how you have honored your wedding vows to him/her. Part of communication and conflict resolution is learning to respectfully verbalize your needs and desires, and to initiate asking forgiveness. Then seek ways to meet the needs of your spouse—and act on them. If your marriage is on shaky ground, seek support and counsel. Approach a couple whose marriage you admire and ask them to mentor you. Consider how the break up of your family would affect future generations. Remember that the same God who made His Son come alive again can resurrect a dead marriage. Marital stress during parenthood is typical. Take action to become marriage builders as you shape the next generation.

---

[1]Josh McDowell, *Right from Wrong* (Dallas: Word, 1994), 292.

For Further Support
* Crabb, Larry. *The Marriage Builder.* Grand Rapids, MI: Zondervan, 1982.
* Rainey, Dennis. *Lonely Husbands, Lonely Wives.* Dallas: Word, 1992.
* Freeman, Becky. *Marriage 911.* Nashville: Broadman & Holman, 1996.
* Smalley, Gary. *Making Love Last Forever.* Nashville: LifeWay Press, 1996.
* Chapman, Gary. *The Five Love Languages.* Chicago: Moody, 1995. Chapman, Gary. *The Five Love Languages Video Pack.* Nashville: LifeWay Press, 1995. *The Five Love Languages Viewer Guide.* Nashville: LifeWay Press, 1995.
* Chapman, Gary. *Building Relationships: A Discipleship Guide for Married Couples.* Nashville: LifeWay Press, 1995. *Building Relationships Leader Guide.* Nashville: LifeWay Press, 1995.
* Chapman, Gary and Betty Hassler. *Communication and Intimacy: Covenant Marriage, Couple's Guide.* Nashville: LifeWay Press, 1992. *Communication and Intimacy: Covenant Marriage Leader's Notebook.* Nashville: LifeWay Press, 1992.
* Garland, Diana and Betty Hassler. *Covenant Marriage: Partnership and Commitment, Couple's Guide.* Nashville: LifeWay Press, 1987. *Covenant Marriage: Partnership and Commitment, Leader's Notebook.* Nashville: LifeWay Press, 1988.

Other Resources for Parents

- *HomeLife. Living with Teenagers. ParentLife.* Monthly magazines for families. Nashville: Sunday School Board of the Southern Baptist Convention.
- Christian Sex Education Series
  Hester, Jimmy; compiler. *Christian Sex Education: Parents and Church Leaders Guide.* Nashville: LifeWay Press, 1995.
  Stevens, Norma. *My Body and Me.* Nashville: Family Touch, 1993.
  Chambers, Ellen. *Boys and Girls: Alike and Different.* Nashville: Family Touch, 1993.
  Lanford, Susan. *Sex! What's That?* Nashville: Family Touch, 1993.
  Cannon, Ann. *Sexuality: God's Gift.* Nashville: Family Touch, 1993.
- Mitchell, Dr. William and Michael A. Mitchell. *Building Strong Families.* Nashville: Broadman & Holman, 1997.
- Building Strong Families Emphasis. Nashville: LifeWay Press, 1997 & 1998.
  Mitchell, Dr. William and Jimmy Hester. *Building Strong Families Leader Guide.*
  Mitchell, Dr. William. *Building Strong Families Leader Kit.*
  Mitchell, Dr. William and Mikey Thomas Oldham. *Peace in the Family.*
  Mitchell, Dr. William and Phyllis Belew. *Self-Control in the Family.*
  Mitchell, Dr. William and Wanda Fulbright King. *Kindness in the Family.*
- Crase, Dixie Ruth and Arthur H. Criscoe. *Parenting by Grace: Discipline and Spiritual Growth, Parent's Guide.* Nashville: LifeWay Press, 1988. *Parenting by Grace: Discipline and Spiritual Growth, Leader's Guide.* Nashville: LifeWay Press, 1996.
- Dobson, James. *Hide or Seek.* Old Tappan, NJ: Fleming H. Revell Company, 1974.
- Dobson, James. *The Strong-Willed Child.* Wheaton, IL: Tyndale House, 1992.
- Farrar, Steve. *Point Man.* Portland: Multnomah, 1990.
- Freeman, Becky and Ruthie Arnold. *Adult Children of Fairly Functional Parents.* Nashville: Broadman & Holman, 1995.
- Kimmel, Tim. *Little House on the Freeway: Help for the Hurried Home.* Sisters, OR: Multnomah, 1994.
- Kjos, Brent. *Your Child and the New Age.* Colorado Springs: Chariot Victor, 1989.
- McDowell, Josh and Bob Hostetler. *Right from Wrong: What You Need to Know to Help Youth Make Right Choices.* Dallas: Word, 1994.
- McDowell, Josh. *Truth Matters … For You and Tomorrow's Generation Adult Workbook.* Nashville: World Bridge Press, 1995. *Truth Matters … For You and Tomorrow's Generation Leader Guide.* Nashville: World Bridge Press, 1995.
- Morgan, Robert. *Empowered Parenting.* Nashville: LifeWay Press, 1996.
- Murray, Andrew. *How to Raise Your Children for Christ.* Minneapolis: Bethany House, 1975.
- Peel, Kathy. *The Family Manager.* Dallas: Word, 1996
- Ramsey, Dave. *Financial Peace.* New York: Viking Penguin, 1997.
- Turecki, Stanley. *The Difficult Child.* New York: Bantam Books, 1989.

CHRISTIAN GROWTH STUDY PLAN

Preparing Christians to Serve

In the **Christian Growth Study Plan (formerly Church Study Course)**, this book *Shaping the Next Generation* is a resource for course credit in the subject area HOME/FAMILY of the Christian Growth category of diploma plans. To receive credit, read the book, complete the learning activities, show your work to your pastor, a staff member or church leader, then complete the following information. This page may be duplicated. Send the completed page to:

Christian Growth Study Plan
127 Ninth Avenue, North, MSN 117
Nashville, TN 37234-0117
FAX: (615)251-5067

For information about the Christian Growth Study Plan, refer to the current Christian Growth Study Plan Catalog. Your church office may have a copy. If not, request a free copy from the Christian Growth Study Plan office (615/251-2525).

Shaping the Next Generation
COURSE NUMBER: CG-0430

PARTICIPANT INFORMATION

Social Security Number (USA ONLY)	Personal CGSP Number*	Date of Birth (MONTH, DAY, YEAR)
— —	—	— —

Name (First, Middle, Last)		Home Phone
☐ Mr. ☐ Miss		
☐ Mrs. ☐		— —

Address (Street, Route, or P.O. Box)	City, State, or Province	Zip/Postal Code

CHURCH INFORMATION

Church Name		
Address (Street, Route, or P.O. Box)	City, State, or Province	Zip/Postal Code

CHANGE REQUEST ONLY

☐ Former Name		
☐ Former Address	City, State, or Province	Zip/Postal Code
☐ Former Church	City, State, or Province	Zip/Postal Code

Signature of Pastor, Conference Leader, or Other Church Leader	Date

*New participants are requested but not required to give SS# and date of birth. Existing participants, please give CGSP# when using SS# for the first time. Thereafter, only one ID# is required. **Mail to: Christian Growth Study Plan, 127 Ninth Ave., North, Nashville, TN 37234-0117. Fax: (615)251-5067**